WICKED WOMEN
of ALABAMA

WICKED WOMEN
of ALABAMA

JEREMY W. GRAY

THE
History
PRESS

Published by The History Press
Charleston, SC
www.historypress.com

Front cover: (*Top image, horizontal*) Marie Hilley's eyes peering over her arm. *From* Alabama's 20th Century Outlaw Women: Murderers, Mobsters, and a Mummy, *photographer Jeremy W. Gray*. (*Bottom image*) The mummy Hazel Farris stretched out on a table. *Courtesy of the* Anniston Star, *from the Alabama Media Group*.

Back cover: (*Top image, horizontal*) Judith Ann Neelley escorted into court. *Courtesy of the Alabama Media Group*. (*Bottom image, horizontal*) Rhonda Bell Martin lighting a cigarette in jail. *Courtesy of the Alabama Media Group*.

First published 2021

Manufactured in the United States

ISBN 9781467146012

Library of Congress Control Number: 2021934107

Notice: The information in this book is true and complete to the best of our knowledge. It is offered without guarantee on the part of the author or The History Press. The author and The History Press disclaim all liability in connection with the use of this book.

CONTENTS

Introduction   7

1. Hazel Farris: Bessemer's Pistol-Packing Mummy   11
2. The Death of Louise Wooster: The Madam Who Saved
    Birmingham from Cholera   19
3. Virginia Hill: Alabama's Mob Queen   31
4. The Puzzling Cases of Alabama's Four 1950s Poisoners   45
5. Two Women, Six Murdered Children: The Mattie Smarr
    and Pearl Griffin Murders   71
6. The Torso Murderer Viola Hyatt   79
7. Patricia Krenwinkel: Mobile's Manson Family Murderer   89
8. Marie Hilley: The Black Widow of Anniston   99
9. Judith Ann Neelley: The Drain Cleaner Killer   110
10. Betty Wilson: Huntsville's Twin Sister Doctor Killer   126
11. Lynda Lyon Block: Alabama's Antigovernment Cop Killer   140

About the Author   157

INTRODUCTION

Drunk, angry and armed with a shotgun, Silena Gilmore walked two blocks from her sister's Birmingham apartment back to the Union Café on Third Avenue North to settle with the young man working behind the counter, who, minutes earlier, had shown Silena to the door when she disturbed other diners. Horace Johnson, a twenty-year-old who left his home in the Cleburne County town on Heflin for Birmingham, on May 6, 1929, told Silena to "stop the racket" and then made her leave the café.

Witnesses said Silena soon returned and watched as Johnson dropped to his knees, raised his hands over his head and begged for his life. Silena shot him dead, they said. She was arrested early the next morning, indicted on a murder charge that same day, stood trial on June 10, 1929, and was convicted the next day after a jury spent forty minutes deliberating. The trial took place thirty-five days after Johnson's murder. Soon followed by a death sentence, the trial was one of the "speediest" in Jefferson County, according to the *Birmingham News*. When the verdict was read, Gilmore beat the table and screamed and then prayed quietly. A bailiff took her out of the courtroom.

As 1930 began, Silena was destined to make history as the first woman to die in Alabama's electric chair, the Big Yellow Mama. Silena was one of four women to die there between 1927, when Alabama abandoned hanging for electrocution, and 2002, when the state retired the electric chair in favor of lethal injection.

THE BIRTH OF THE BIG YELLOW MAN

After gambling away his money in New Orleans, British-born ca
Edward Mason was convicted of burglarizing six homes in Mobile
"I entered the homes without a gun and in daytime....I never in
doing anyone bodily harm," Mason later told the *Birmingham News*. Ma
may not have intended to hurt anyone while carrying out his crimes, but in
seeking to reduce his twelve- to sixty-year sentence, Mason helped send 177
of his fellow inmates to their deaths over the course of seventy-five years.

Mason worked alone to build a 150-pound maple wood chair with
adjustable arms and headrest; no other inmates would even help carry the
lumber. "Every stroke of the saw meant liberty to me, and the fact that it
would aid in bringing death to others didn't occur to me," Mason said. The
state engineer installed electrical wiring on Mason's chair, and it was painted
in the same garish yellow that lines state roads. It wasn't just the paint job
that earned the chair its name—many of the condemned thought the chair
was reuniting them with their dead mothers. Instead of bringing Mason
freedom, the work filled his cell with nightmares. "I've been haunted,"
Mason told a reporter. "I haven't been able to sleep much at night."

"I have made cradles and caskets, but this is my first electric chair. And if I
were called upon to make another, I would flatly refuse and pay the penalty.
It could be no worse than a troubled conscience," Mason said in 1927. That
was the year that convicted double murderer Horace DeVaughn was the
first to die of his creation. The state engineer who installed the wiring on
Mason's chair was supposed to throw the switch, but they quit days before
the scheduled execution. It took four jolts of electricity and twelve minutes
before DeVaughn was dead. Mason eventually left prison and the state,
supposedly forever, although it is not clear when that happened.

Mason's electric chair ended the lives of thirteen other men over the
next two years. With Gilmore set to become the first woman to die in
the state electric chair, sixty-nine people, on behalf of groups of reform-
minded Black women, pleaded with the state pardon board to commute
her sentence. "Alabama has made great progress along all lines under your
administration and should continue to do so but cannot by resorting to the
inhumane processes of the Middle Ages," wrote one of those organizations,
the Twentieth Century Club, according to the *Montgomery Advertiser*. Governor
Bibb Graves let the execution sentence stand.

On January 24, 1930, Gilmore "marched to her death, singing," according
to the *Cleburne News* in Heflin, Johnson's hometown. "I'm here because c

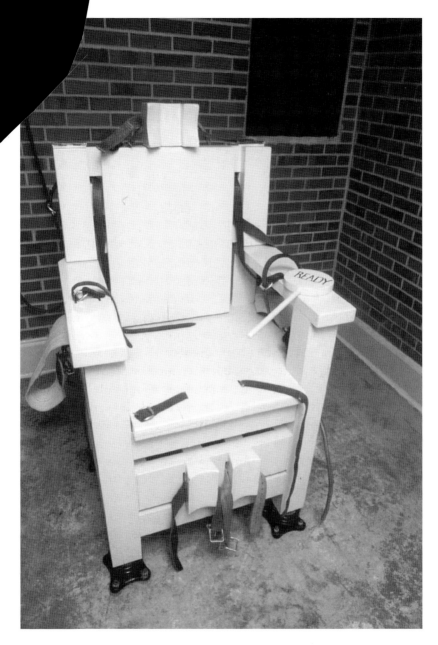

Alabama's electric chair, the Big Yellow Mama, with matching paddle stating "READY." The paddle was used by an attendant in the death chamber to signal the executioner when it was time to throw the switch. *Courtesy of the* Huntsville Times.

corn and canned heat," Gilmore said in an apparent reference [...] liquor that inspired more than a few songs. The first jolt hit Gil[...] a.m. She was pronounced dead two jolts later, at 12:14 a.m. Gil[...] first woman executed in Alabama since an 1888 hanging in Bulloc[...] and she was the first woman to be executed in the state's electric ch[...] put that into context, Alabama electrocuted five men in a span of forty-se[...] minutes early one February morning in 1934. In fact, only a little more than 2.25 percent of those who died in Alabama's electric chair between 1927 and 2002 were women. The last person to die in the chair in Alabama, as of this writing, was a woman.

Men commit the greatest number of crimes and fill most prisons. As of this writing, 83 men are awaiting execution by lethal injection in Alabama, although state law gives the condemned the option to bring the electric out of retirement if that's how they wish to die. As of this writing, 5 women are facing execution in Alabama, and some 23,500 men and 2,300 women are Alabama prison inmates.

Despite all of this, in the twentieth century, there were a number of stories, many of doubtful origin, of women seeking to escape poverty through crime. There are tales of women who poisoned for profit and pleasure and of women linked to some of the nation's most heinous crimes of the 1900s—even as far away as California—who had Alabama ties. Theirs are stories of brutal axe murders and profound injustices, and they were often played out in newspapers with prominent remarks about the physical appearances of female suspects that infamous male criminals were never forced to endure. Some of the stories ended in executions, mental hospitals and mysteries.

When writing this book, I attempted to contact as many of the living as I could, writing to the convicted women in prison and tracking down those who walk free, forever in the shadow of these tragic crimes. Now, more than twenty years after the end of the twentieth century and long since many of the women who were involved were either sent to the grave or put behind prison walls, these tales live on. For many who were touched by the crimes, their scars will never fade.

As Silena Gilmore supposedly said on her dying day, "Crime does not pay."

1

HAZEL FARRIS

Bessemer's Pistol-Packing Mummy

azel Farris barely survived her first forty years on the road. Visiting forty-eight states between 1911 and 1950, people paid to see her at county fairs and town squares, and she was publicly examined by local doctors. While greeting crowds in a Carthage, Tennessee movie theater lobby, someone snatched a gold tooth from Hazel's mouth. So many people touched Hazel's hand for good luck, her bones began to wear through the skin. And then there was the time that Hazel's coffin, her resting place between shows, slid out of the back of a truck, onto a lonesome highway. Dead since 1906, the mummy Hazel Farris, her strange visage frozen in time, was as resilient as she was popular.

Hazel's death and life inspired stories I heard at sleepovers growing up in Bessemer, Alabama, in the 1980s and 1990s. My brother had a teacher who wanted Hazel exposed to radiation at the Browns Ferry Nuclear Plant in Athens to ensure that she would always be fit for display.

So, how does one become a mummy, and why are we talking about Hazel Farris 115 years after she died?

It all began in Louisville, Kentucky, on the morning of August 6, 1905, when Hazel shot and killed her husband after he refused to allow her to buy a new hat. The shot was heard by three police officers who were walking to a nearby station house. The lawmen rushed into the couple's home and saw Hazel standing over her murdered husband. Hazel quickly took aim, and the three officers were soon dead, lying on the floor alongside Hazel's husband.

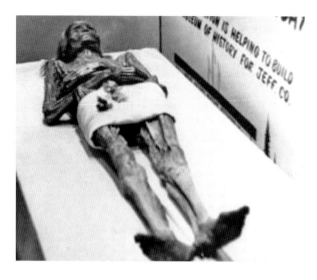

The remains of Hazel Farris were put on display to raise funds for the Bessemer Hall of History in 1974. *Courtesy of www.Bhamwiki.com.*

Hazel hid inside the house while a deputy sheriff who had been summoned by neighbors crept into the home. "His stealth was no match for her reflexes or deadly marksmanship," folklorist and former University of Alabama professor Dr. Elaine Katz wrote in her 1978 book *Folklore for the Time of Your Life.* Hazel and the deputy struggled, and the deputy shot Hazel's right ring finger off just moments before she fired a shot of her own and made him her fifth victim. Hazel fled down an alley, blood gushing from her hand, finally settling in Bessemer as a $500,000 reward was posted for the twenty-six-year-old killer of five.

Once in Bessemer, Hazel either taught school or was a sex worker, depending on which account you believe. Either way, Hazel had a huge appetite for whiskey and found comfort in the arms of a Bessemer police officer. On December 20, 1906, when Hazel told her lover of her deadly past in Kentucky, he turned her in. "Over a bottle of whiskey, she made the decision not to submit to arrest. She took her own life by ingesting poison—arsenic or strychnine, the very chemicals that were once used as embalming fluids (before such use was made illegal in order to keep poison murders from going undetected)," Katz wrote.

There's just one big problem—none of that happened.

I have searched for years and never have I seen one newspaper article about a woman in Kentucky mercilessly killing five people in 1905, losing a finger in the process, and then dying by suicide as police closed in on her. A historian once said he suspected it just wasn't reported at the time. I don't buy it.

The newspaper business in the early 1900s was a tank full of starving sharks chasing a lone goldfish. In cities and towns, numerous newspapers published multiple editions each day, all in a fight to the death as poverty-stricken children shouted headlines from street corners. There is no way in hell a story like Hazel Farris's wouldn't have made front pages from Andalusia to Anchorage. I asked Dr. Katz if she thought the story was true. "It wasn't necessary to know if it's true," Katz said with a laugh. "It was a wonderful legend. It was like a ghost story."

If anyone in Alabama knows a great story, it's Elaine Katz. Her father was the rabbi who performed the marriage ceremony for Anne Frank's parents. Her parents later fled Europe and settled in Selma. She watched Governor George Wallace stand in the schoolhouse door at the University of Alabama (UA) in 1963. Years later, with the help of her friend Kathryn Tucker Windham, the author of the legendary *13 Alabama Ghosts and Jeffrey* and one of my earliest influences, Katz brought Hazel to the UA campus. "We treated her with respect," Katz recalled.

This photograph, purported to have been taken before the death of Hazel Farris, was often used in a handbill advertising an appearance by the mummy. *From Folklore for the Time of Your Life by Elaine Katz.*

"HAZEL MUST PAY FOR HER ERRORS"

According to legend, Hazel was taken to a Bessemer furniture store until a family member could claim her body. No one ever did, and the store owner noticed that folks were willing to pay to see Hazel's corpse, which wasn't decomposing, though her body weight shrunk from 106 pounds to just 37 pounds. "Most of the usual signs of physical deterioration were not occurring," Katz wrote. "Hazel's body had somehow dehydrated to enter a state of mummification."

Hazel soon went to a Tuscaloosa furniture store, where Olanda Clayton Brooks, a traveling carnival man, bought her corpse for twenty-five dollars. Brooks's great-nephew Luther Brooks told Katz, "He put her in the garage at my granddaddy's house. And he went to Louisville, Kentucky, and

Luther Brooks smiles as he poses with Hazel Farris. *Courtesy of the* Tennessean.

stayed there for five years, researching to see if she had any relatives. He didn't find any at all. That's when he came back to Nashville and started showing Hazel."

In the first twelve days that Hazel was on display on Nashville's Church Street in 1911, eighteen thousand people paid to see her. O.C. Brooks then carried Hazel across America and even into Europe. During weeklong fairs, O.C. Brooks would keep Hazel in hiding until Friday and Saturday; he would spend the preceding days walking the midway, yelling for folks to come back and see "one of the wonders of the world." Hazel was always a star attraction.

The years of travel took a toll on Hazel. A Louisiana journalist spread the claim that touching her hand brought good luck, so O.C. Brooks charged extra during afterhours shows for those who were eager to pay to touch the mummy's hand. "The skeletal structure of her hand became exposed," Katz wrote.

O.C. Brooks died penniless in 1950, although his family said he made nearly $250 a week during the Great Depression by propping Hazel up on street corners and charging people a nickel to see her. "If he didn't drink it up or gamble it, I don't know what he done with it because he was the poorest of the poor," Luther Brooks told Katz. O.C. supposedly bequeathed Hazel to his family, and they found her remains under the bed in O.C.'s one-room Louisiana shack—he had been sleeping on top of her coffin for years. O.C.'s will supposedly stated, "Never sell her or show her as a freak, and never bury her. Hazel must pay for her errors, and I must pay for mine. If you ever show her, you must donate all the money to charity; for I did not, and it should be in the name of science and education, for Hazel is a medical wonder."

"I'VE NEVER USED HAZEL TO SCARE PEOPLE"

Hazel made a few later appearances to raise funds for politicians, schools and churches, Luther told the *Tennessean* in 1960. But Luther all but stopped showing Hazel in public in 1964, though she was sometimes displayed to raise funds for the Bessemer Hall of History.

One of Katz's students, my old friend James "Doc" Walker, helped care for Hazel. He was an artist who performed music for fellow soldiers in Korea, and his history column ran in Bessemer's *Western Star* newspaper during my cub reporter days there. Caring for Hazel included annual treatments with warm water and washing powder. Her corpse was insured for $150,000 and was rigged with an alarm system. "I wish that Hazel could be put in a beautiful place and shown so that dust and stuff wouldn't get on her, and I think she'll be here for generations to come as an important part of science," Walker told Katz. Doc died in 2007.

Nothing could stop the process of Hazel's decomposition forever. O.C., in his final years, had taken to calling her "Hazel, the (no longer) beautiful." When Hazel went on display in Samson, Alabama, in 1911, a newspaper said her "hair [was] soft and pliant as that of a child's and is now eight inches longer than at the time of her death. Her fingernails grow, and perspiration appears from time to time." In just twenty years, all of that began to change. "Pathologists are unable to explain why Hazel's mummified body remained

She Was A Pistol Packin' Mama

By PHILLIP RAWLS
Of the Advertiser Staff

BESSEMER — Her steel nerve, deadly aim, and mummified body have made
Hazel Farris famous for some 70 years after

According to a Bessemer historian,
Jim Walker, corpses in those days (1906)
were taken to furniture stores, which did
embalming and sold caskets.
Hazel's public repose attracts thou-
sion-Adams store in downtown Besse-

apparently diminished, and her owner
died in poverty about 30 years ago in
Louisiana. The owner had a young nephew in Nashville, Tenn., and he willed
"Hazel the (no longer) Beautiful" to the
nephew with the stipulation that she nev-

This cartoon depicts the alleged Kentucky murders of Hazel Farris. Courtesy of the Montgomery Advertiser.

beautiful until 1931, when she began to age. Her skin turned bronze and leathery, and her hair began to recede," legendary Alabama journalist Phillip Rawls wrote in 1976.

Hazel also suffered some strange mishaps. She was sometimes soaked by snow and rain that slipped through a window of the building she was stored in. "We kept her locked in a pine box when I was in school, and one day, I jumped on the box catching a ball—broke her nose," Luther Brooks told the *Tennessean*. "Another rain-slick night, Hazel, pine box and all, slid from the trunk of the car onto the highway, but we just slid her back in and went on." Surviving each calamity, Luther prepared Hazel for each busy season, usually around Halloween, with a treatment of "embalming fluid, dry wash and a hose pipe shower." He decorated her coffin with fluorescent lights and artificial grass. Her later public appearances were described as Hazel "repaying her debt to society."

When Luther Brooks brought Hazel back to Bessemer in 1994, she had not been seen there since 1985. "I've never used Hazel to scare people or nothing," Brooks told the *Birmingham News* at the time. "I've only let the Bessemer Hall of History take her because she killed herself down there."

"SHE WAS NOTORIOUS AND IGNORED"

Museum supporter Joel Mulkin drove to Franklin, Tennessee, to get Hazel, and he carried her lifeless body through the night back to Alabama. "I was more scared about getting pulled over by police," Mulkin told the *Birmingham News*. "I don't think I'd make a very good mortician. I was ready to get rid of Hazel this morning."

Hazel, all thirty-three pounds of her, was displayed with her arms crossed over her chest and her lower body draped with a white cloth. "She is a little anorexic at present," museum supporter Ed Kean told the *Birmingham News* while helping prepare Hazel. "Some people think it is really gross to show her, and I guess it might be, but it's a part of Bessemer history and that's what we're here for."

"It's her way of paying for her earlier sins in life," museum supporter Louise Ayer Tommie told the *Birmingham News*. About seven hundred people, paying one dollar for kids to enter and two dollars for adults, visited Hazel at the Bessemer Hall of History during a ten-day stay in the city that autumn, including three busloads of school kids in a single day. "The thing I noticed most were there were people who had seen her before who brought their children back," Tommie said.

As Hazel made her way back to Franklin, Tennessee, Brooks told the *Birmingham News* he might continue to use Hazel to raise money for a good cause. "God breathed into you and gave you a soul. It doesn't matter what you do to a body," Luther Brooks once said. "I've never seen anything wrong with it as long as you don't fool with the soul of a person."

In 2001, the National Geographic Channel's *The Mummy Road Show* visited Hazel's final owner, a woman they identified only as Teresa. The show's hosts, Drs. Ronald Beckett and Jerry Conlogue, examined Hazel with an X-ray and endoscope, and they took her to Vanderbilt University for a full body scan and Oklahoma for a full autopsy. The two awestruck professors watched as Hazel was sawed into pieces and her organs exposed for the world to see.

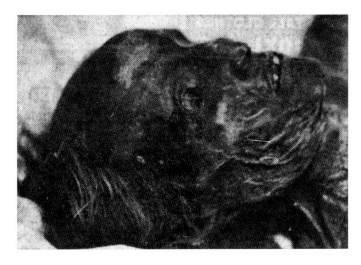

An old news clipping showing a closeup look of the mummified face of Hazel Farris. *Courtesy of the* Birmingham News.

Sometime after that autopsy, Hazel was cremated. She was nearly put to her final rest before she could be examined by the National Geographic Channel. "I believed that Hazel's 'owner' was somewhat conflicted. She thought it was time for the remains to be buried. However, we convinced her to allow us to do an autopsy," Conlogue told me. He and Beckett believe Hazel's mummification was the result of her embalmment, not the manner of her death. "It would not be possible to ingest a sufficient quantity of 'poison' to preserve an entire body. Hazel was definitely embalmed shortly after her death," Conlogue said. "There was no way this was a poisoning case. Hazel was embalmed with arsenic," Beckett added.

And what of the sordid story of Hazel Farris's brief life that attracted so many crowds? Could any of it have been true? "Hazel had quite a story written about her, designed to draw people into the sideshow tent," Beckett recalled. "We hoped to try to give her back some identity, which we could not do completely. However, the response to our efforts was received well by Hazel's 'owner,' who really wanted her treated with respect. The entire sense from this around us was that people wanted to know more about this mummified woman."

The Mummy Road Show's producer, Larry Engle, told the *Tennessean* in 2002 that, while Hazel "probably died alone, an outcast, derelict, stranger," there was no truth to the tales of murder and suicide. "The autopsy told us that the legend was really nothing more than a legend." Katz told me, "She was notorious and ignored. I'm sure it was rough. I'm sure she was witness to rough living, if not participating. Roughnecks didn't care who they raped, and the cops didn't care either. I don't know if she was a good girl or a bad girl."

2

THE DEATH OF LOUISE WOOSTER

The Madam Who Saved Birmingham from Cholera

Louise Wooster's troubled life came to a quiet end on May 16, 1913, in the Birmingham house that was paid for by the toil of the women she employed as sex workers. Madam Lou died in the city she helped save in its infancy from cholera forty years earlier, a city that loved her, as she had made a fortune selling her body and the bodies of others. Madam Wooster's life of crime began perhaps as a necessity, born out of a desire to escape poverty and lift those she loved from the ravages of life in 1800s Alabama.

After her death from the kidney-destroying Bright's disease, Wooster's funeral was held at her home at 1909 Avenue D. She was buried at Oak Hill Cemetery, along with her family members who had preceded her in death, the women who worked for her and their babies. Those employees and infants might have otherwise been buried in a pauper's field.

For all her sorrow, the seventy-year-old left behind a life of legend, including a dubious romance with one of America's most hated assassins, a rumored inspiration for *Gone with the Wind*'s Belle Watling, and tales of customers' empty carriages following her to the grave. Lou's clients may have loved her but not enough to risk the shame of showing their faces at her funeral. By the time of her death, Wooster was a Birmingham legend who had amassed wealth for her family by exploiting young women in the same fashion she had been used as a teenager. What choice did she have? She was a motherless child in the 1850s trying to save her sisters. "Over my life, there hung a shadow," she wrote in her memoir. "I could not cast off the feeling

Artist Max Heldman's depiction of Birmingham madam Louise Wooster. *Courtesy of* Max Heldman's Birmingham.

that I was doomed to disappointment, sorrow and despair."

When the "terrible cholera scourge of '73" came, half of Birmingham's 4,000 residents fled, and 128 of those who stayed behind died. Unlike many of those who stayed, Wooster said she had the means to stay and help, although she feared that a prostitute's offer to tend the sick and dying would be refused. Instead, Wooster's help was warmly received. "Wherever I went to nurse, whether to the comfortable home or the hovel, I was kindly accepted by rich and poor alike," she wrote. "My doors were thrown open to the homeless ones. My purse strings were loosened, and all that I had to give was for those in need."

Wooster, however, said nothing of her occupation and was not seeking the gratitude she earned in 1873, which lives on nearly 150 years later. "I little dreamed and little cared for the reputation I had made, never thinking I had done more than my duty and feeling that if I died at my post that would, in a measure, atone for my sins. I did not fear death; I rather courted it."

"No Time for Tears"

Louise Catherine Wooster was born in Tuscaloosa to William and Mary Chism Wooster on June 12, 1842, according to historian Ellin Sterne Jimmerson. The family had moved to Mobile by the time Louise was seven. She was the fifth youngest of eight daughters, wrote historian Donna Causey. Louise's father was an engineer from New York, and her mother was a native of South Carolina. Wooster described herself as having a proud family lineage, full of rich relatives who would not acknowledge her existence.

When William died in 1851, Wooster's mother married John Williams, according to Causey. "Lou's stepfather took all their money and left the family to fend for themselves. Her mother died a few years later, and as so many young children were, Lou was left an orphan with nothing to rely on but the mercy of relatives," Causey wrote. Wooster couldn't rely on that at all.

By the time she was a teenager, Wooster had been orphaned, abused and abandoned. Her sisters were placed in Mobile's Protestant Orphan Asylum against her mother's wishes the day after her 1857 funeral. Wooster was then preyed on by a callous brother-in-law and family friend, the future Confederate major Robert A. Harris, who sexually manipulated the child. Wooster blamed herself for the ugly actions of that predator, writing that she yielded "to his seductive powers." Harris's greatest sin, she wrote, was his refusal to make her a child bride. "One more was added to the already too full ranks of the lost.…He had accomplished his hellish desires—what more did he want or care?"

When she was stricken with yellow fever, Wooster, then homeless, nearly joined her parents in a Mobile graveyard. The teen had fallen "beyond redemption" when she was taken to a brothel and nursed back to health by "poor unfortunates" who had been driven to prostitution by "cruel treatment" from their husbands, she wrote. Those women taught Wooster two lessons: she would have to embrace a life of sin to save her sisters from the orphanage, and Alabama's most wretched sinners were often its greatest saints. "There was no time for tears," she wrote. "My sisters shall not stay in that place. I will have them out."

Her First Sin

After their mother's death, one of Wooster's older sisters, Margaret, became a sex worker, according to Causey. "Margaret married several times and eventually owned a brothel in Birmingham on 3rd Avenue North, under the name of 'Maggie Bracken.'" For a while, Lou lived with another older sister, Frances, in New Orleans. According to Causey, when Frances's husband refused to take in her younger sisters from the orphanage, Wooster took a ship back to Mobile and forged a letter in her sister Frances's handwriting, claiming she sent Lou to fetch the girls because Frances was too ill to travel.

Wooster later called that forged letter her first sin. "If a sin it was, a just and good God will, I know, forgive me," she wrote.

It was after Wooster retrieved her sisters that she returned to Harris in Mobile. It was then Harris abandoned Lou and left her to die until prostitutes saved her life and set her on her own criminal path. Wooster settled at a Montgomery brothel to spare her dead parents' reputation in Mobile. There, she said she became a favorite of the house's other "inmates"—a term used at the time to describe the women who lived and worked in such places. "I tried to cultivate all that was good in me and crush out all that was degrading. Though the brightest jewel had been plucked from my little crown, I had been determined to keep all of my other good qualities bright and untarnished."

Although she dreamed of a better future in Montgomery, Wooster was unable to escape the death, despair and disappointment she had known all her short life. She was also destined to be linked throughout her life to one of America's greatest tragedies.

"Had the Devil Not Tempted Him"

As the clouds of slavery and a brewing war shrouded the state capital, Wooster claimed to have had an affair with doomed young actor John Wilkes Booth. There is little evidence to support this or the claim she made years later to newspapers that Booth had not been killed. Jimmerson wrote, "Her remarkable claim of an affair with John Wilkes Booth, undocumented outside her interviews and autobiography, presents her as the true love of America's heart-throb leading man prior to his assassination of Lincoln and, thus, as a supporting actor in one of the most significant events in American history."

"Handsome, generous, affectionate and brave," Wooster wrote of Booth. "He was my ideal man." She even claimed he wanted her to pursue a career in theater. "Then we would always be together—no need of a separation ever again."

Booth began performing at the Montgomery Theater in the winter of 1860, the *Montgomery Advertiser* reported in a 1920 article. "He was the hardest drinker of the crowd of hard drinkers," the paper wrote. "Once on the stage, he was a transformed man; his natural genius as an actor lifted him above the rather primitive environment of the old stage fittings of that day, and he stood out in the cast of any play." Confederate Captain J.V. Ashurst told the newspaper he once saw Booth at a party, sullen and drunk as others sang and laughed. The crowd called for Booth to perform for them. "He was then so intoxicated, or so nearly intoxicated, that he had to steady himself by holding the edge of the table. He threw back his long black hair, and with his pale face turned upward, he recited the Lord's Prayer. He did nothing else. He said nothing else." The men were brought to tears. Booth sank back in his chair and buried his face in his hands.

Wooster wrote that she was heartbroken when Booth told her he had to leave her and would send for her soon. "Such a glorious country as ours can not [*sic*] be broken up by a few fanatics," she said he told her. "All will be over in a few weeks." She said she replied, "I will never see you again. This is our final parting."

Wooster wrote that Booth loved the Union and said his "strange, erratic nature" that fateful night he gunned down President Lincoln at the Ford's Theatre was the result of him "crazed by drink." She said that he believed his "terrible act" would end the war and save the South. "Had the devil not tempted him at that fatal moment, what a bright star would he have been....I knew he was impulsive, erratic, but I never believed him capable of murder. I do not believe he ever intended murder....Though the world may condemn him, I love him still." In her later years, Wooster was known to keep a scrapbook full of mementos about Booth, including a monogrammed handkerchief and several letters, Causey wrote.

Wooster claimed that when her relationship with Booth ended, she performed as an actress in Arkansas and New Orleans. After surviving tuberculosis, she quit the stage and, in 1869, moved back to Mobile, Causey wrote. Wooster wrote that she eventually agreed to marry a man she called John Pollak (likely a pseudonym). The engagement supposedly ended in bloodshed before wedding bells could ever ring. "Many Montgomerians will remember that day in January when John Pollak was cruelly, foully murdered by a crowd of drunken, bloodthirsty ruffians." He was shot in the door of the Exchange Hotel and died a few hours later. And just like that, Wooster was back where she had started.

Wooster turned again to prostitution and went back to Mobile, where she met a man she called Frank. She wrote that he lost money gambling and began to drink. When he finally lost everything, Wooster said she went back to Montgomery and used the money men paid her for sex to send her sister Nellie to a prestigious Tennessee boarding school. She wrote that she lied to the school to get Nellie in—she told them her money had come from acting.

"The City was Dead"

It was around this time that the Magic City, incorporated in 1871, caught Wooster's eye.

> *It was, at that time, a railroad crossing with a little town of about twenty or thirty houses, and very poor houses, at that. The papers throughout the state were full of Birmingham, and very soon, I became absorbed in it myself.…A town not over one year old, but to see the business and bustle here was truly wonderful. All was life, and money was plentiful.*

Wooster had only been in Birmingham a few months when cholera hit. "Every one [*sic*] who could possibly leave the stricken little city lost no time in getting away. Those who were too poor and had not the means to go, those whose duty forbade them fleeing the danger and a few brave and noble ones who were not afraid to face danger, were all of the well ones left behind." Wooster had the means to leave. Friends told her she would die if she stayed. "Why I remained has always been a mystery to me," she wrote. "I was determined to stay and help nurse the poor sick and suffering ones who needed me."

When the epidemic was over, the city was in ruins. "You could buy all of Birmingham now for less money than, in years during the 'boom,' it would have taken to buy a single block. The city was dead but not my infatuation." And Birmingham, too, was infatuated with her. When an ex-lover she called the "Montgomery tyrant" followed her to Birmingham, her friends told him she was protected and put him on a train out of town.

In the 1880s, according to Jimmerson, Wooster bought a two-story home on Fourth Avenue North and an adjacent building that became one of Birmingham's "high-class" brothels. Jimmerson wrote:

> *Near city hall, saloons, and the police station, the location offered Wooster access to influence, customers, alcohol, and police protection. She continued to prosper. By 1887, Wooster's considerable assets included land, buildings, furniture, and jewelry. She held the funeral of at least one of her prostitutes at her brothel. She buried several others and at least two of their infants in her Oak Hill Cemetery plot.*

Wooster lived with seven sex workers and a servant, Causey wrote. "The next year, she purchased the building next to hers. She and her youngest

The buildings in this image, once occupied by Alabama Barber College (*left center*) and Alabama Supply Company (*right center*) on Birmingham's Fourth Avenue North, housed the brothel that was owned by Louise Wooster during the 1880s. *Courtesy of the Birmingham Public Library Archives.*

sister, Cornelia, and her sickly son lived in one building, while she operated a brothel in another."

Wooster became a well-known philanthropist and storyteller. The *Birmingham Age Newspaper*, in 1887, listed Wooster among those who were pledging one hundred dollars to a charity hospital campaign. Wooster, in later years, however, whitewashed the ugly realities of life and death in Birmingham's red-light district. "Her *autobiography* is devoid of brutal realities of prostitution in Birmingham—its close association with poverty created by the cotton mills that supplied 'high-class' brothels their 'girls' and the young boys who served as night messengers, saloons, violent crime, sexually transmitted diseases, and police graft," Jimmerson wrote.

While Wooster may never have spoken publicly of the "brutal realities of prostitution in Birmingham," she knew them well.

"A Great Injustice Has Been Done Me"

Walter H. Wilson, a guard at the Pratt Mines, where prison inmates toiled, showed up at the door of Wooster's brothel in 1885. Wilson asked Wooster for food for a prisoner there, the notorious Alabama outlaw and former Sumter County sheriff Stephen Renfroe. "I would not refuse anyone that," Wooster later wrote in a letter to the *Birmingham Chronicle*.

Wooster said that she and Wilson discussed trying to get Renfroe a pardon for his many crimes, which included deserting the Confederacy, killing his brother-in-law in a dispute over chickens, beating his wife and terrorizing Black residents as a member of the Ku Klux Klan. Despite his alleged involvement in the disappearance of a judge and the murder of a magistrate's bodyguard, Renfroe was elected sheriff in 1878. Once elected, his list of crimes grew to include arson, assault, blackmail and stealing from his office. He was arrested in 1880.

"Later in the evening, a lady in the house came to me with a pistol in her hand, saying, 'Miss Lou, will you keep this? I am afraid of it,'" Wooster's letter to the *Chronicle* continued. Wooster said the young woman told her, "That man left it with me until he calls for it. He has two and says this one is so heavy he didn't want to bother with it." Wooster said, "I was not supposed to know the gun was stolen, as I had no idea thieves were employed as guards."

Wooster said Wilson later came back with another man, and she questioned Wilson about the gun. She said she later learned the man with Wilson was an official from Pratt Mines. Renfroe had just made the last in a five-year series of escapes. Wooster said she was shocked to hear of the escape and that Wilson had left a stolen gun there for Renfroe. Justus Collins, the manager of convicts at Pratt Mines, wasn't buying it. When *Livingston Journal* editor Frank Herr wrote a romanticized account of a nighttime trek through a swamp in October 1885, hoping to meet his old friend Renfroe, Collins unleashed his fury. Herr wrote that he and other reporters were guided by an armed man who blew on an acorn whistle to signal to Renfroe. They found the former sheriff sitting on a log with a double-barrel shotgun in his lap and Remington revolver on his belt.

"Renfroe cannot be captured," the *Alabama Journal* wrote, "because but one person can see him at a time, and no one man can take him….He has an impregnable position from which he could kill as many men and dogs as might come within reach of him." Collins wrote a letter that was shared by multiple Alabama newspapers, saying Renfroe "went into Birmingham after leaving here for the purpose of finding the house of Lou Wooster, a woman of bad repute," with whom Wilson had left a pistol for the disgraced lawman. "There is no question but Walter H. Wilson, Lou Wooster, and other friends of Renfroe whom I do not know will read the 'interview' with feelings of unalloyed pleasure, but when it comes to be read by law-abiding citizens, it will be read with sadness and regret."

Wooster fired back at Collins with a newspaper account of her own:

I think a great injustice has been done me, and I hope you will print what I have to say in vindication of myself. Justus Collins is either mistaken or

This drawing by cartoonist Charles Brooks depicts the lynching of ex–Sumter County sheriff Stephen Renfroe. *Courtesy of the* Birmingham News.

maliciously did me an injustice. When I knew Renfroe, he was a gentleman whose character was above reproach, and I never knew him after he was accused of crime. Though had I never known him, I could not refuse his piteous appeal for something to eat....I believe my character for truthfulness and honesty can be substantiated by the good people of Birmingham.

Eight months later, on July 13, 1886, Renfroe was marched through the streets of Livingston. He had been recaptured after farmers in Enterprise, Mississippi, blasted him off a stolen mule with a load of squirrel shot. That night, fifteen disguised men overpowered the jailer, took Renfroe out of town and lynched him. "Thus ends the career of the most daring desperate character Alabama ever produced," one newspaper proclaimed.

This would not be the last time Wooster's life was touched by violence

"Sin, Sorrow, Love and Duty"

On January 8, 1894, Birmingham firefighter Ben Stehlin was standing in front of the Nineteenth Street Market when he saw Josie Burke walking by with a strange man following close behind. Burke was a seventeen-year-old native of Hill City, Tennessee, described by the *Birmingham Daily News* as an "inmate of Lou Wooster." The man following Burke was W.B. Buchanan. He had previously tried to walk beside her, but Josie warned that he might be arrested for doing so. She stopped to say hello to Stehlin. "Don't have anything to do with that man," Josie said Buchanan told her. "What have you got to do with it?" she said Stehlin asked Buchanan.

The two kept arguing until Stehlin hit Buchanan with a left hook, and the two started trading punches. Stehlin slugged Buchanan three times in the stomach. Buchanan fell hard to the sidewalk, his head hitting the girl's foot. The two left, "doubtless thinking the man was not badly hurt and would soon arise and go his way," the paper reported. He did not.

A man named William Wise saw Buchanan bleeding in the street and went to a fire station for help. Stehlin helped Wise carry Buchanan into Davidson's pharmacy. Buchanan died minutes later without saying a word. Stehlin was arrested when Burke told the police what happened. "He is a quiet, good-natured fellow, and no one regrets the affair of last night more than he," Josie reportedly said of the firefighter. Stehlin denied hitting Buchanan in the stomach and said Buchanan had brass knuckles. Stehlin said he even used his left hand instead of his right hand because he had hurt his right after hitting a Black woman he saw knock over a White woman at the market a week earlier.

Perhaps tired of being linked to such events, Wooster retired in 1901 and published her fictionalized life story, *The Autobiography of a Magdalen*, ten years later. "Many pages in my life's history are too dark for the public eye; to read them would bring a shudder to the most hardened, the most callous heart. Yet, with all this, my pathway through life has been strewn with flowers compared to thousands of others," she wrote. "Soon, the curtain will drop on the last scene that will hide forever from view sin, sorrow, love and duty."

"WHY SHOULD WOMAN BE PUNISHED MORE THAN MAN?"

After Wooster's curtain fell for the last time in 1913, her legend took on a life of its own.

"With or without facts, Alabamians continue to re-invent Louise Wooster," Jimmerson wrote. "Without evidence, fans insist that for Wooster's funeral, Birmingham's prominent men formed a blocks-long cortege of empty carriages to escort her body to Oak Hill and cherish the doubtful theory that Margaret Mitchell based her *Gone With the Wind* character, Belle Watling, on her."

In 1971, Wooster was featured in a historical drama for Birmingham's centennial celebration. In 2000, Alabama Operaworks commissioned *Louise: The Story of a Magdalen*; in 2004, it won the Nancy Van de Vate International Composition Prize for Opera. In 2007, the Wooster Lofts, the first loft development in Birmingham, was named in her honor. And since 2007, the Lou Wooster Public Health Hero Award has been presented by the Broad Street Committee of the University of Alabama at Birmingham (UAB) School of Public Health to an "unconventional health hero." Honorees are carried from UAB to Oak Hill Cemetery by a horse-drawn carriage for the ceremony.

Wooster, however, would possibly have wanted her legacy to be the testament to the cruel double standard women face when forced to survive in a brutal manmade world. "Treat both sexes alike. Let both be punished or both go free," she wrote. "Why should woman be punished more than man? If charity is to be shown to anyone, let it be the weak woman." She would want her life story to shine a light on the hypocrisy she saw in affluent, Christian women shunning her while penniless prostitutes cared for her when she battled yellow fever and attempted suicide by morphine after a lover she couldn't be seen with in public was shot to death.

The greatest cruelty she said she had ever seen came from so-called Christian women. "Have they ever been thrown on the world at a very tender age with sisters younger than themselves dependent on them for bread? Penniless orphans robbed of all their inheritance by relatives or guardians—not one to hold out a hand to save!" Few, she wrote, were eager to help her leave her "life of shame." "Women must fall. Women must suffer. Women must be punished for their fall. Man can drag a poor woman to her ruin. He can leave his victim a weeping and wailing outcast, while he will be received into the homes of our best, wealthiest and most moral families.... This is what the world calls right and just."

In her later years, Wooster said she was contacted by her father's sister, who had tracked her down from Hartford, Connecticut. Wooster told her aunt everything about her life. "Oh, child, why did you not end your life and that of your little sisters before you marred the beauty of your own soul's virtue," she said her aunt replied.

Wooster seemed to find peace as the twentieth century dawned on Birmingham. "Fortune has favored me, and I have been able to help those who needed help, and it has been a pleasure to me to do so." Madam Wooster said her life had been defined by her "fatal mistake," although it had made her wealthy. She believed there was a heavenly home awaiting her, despite her many sins. "From faith, I gather this: 'The Son of Man is come to save that which was lost.'"

3

VIRGINIA HILL

Alabama's Mob Queen

With her fiery Alabama drawl, Virginia Hill captivated U.S. senators as she testified about America's most notorious gangsters, including her lover, Benjamin "Bugsy" Siegel, who was gunned down in her Beverly Hills mansion.

Millions gathered around TV sets on March 15, 1951, to watch a thirty-four-year-old farm girl in a $5,000 mink stole tell of lavish gifts from infamous mobsters in her televised hearing. Hill said she made more money than she could manage, sometimes $30,000 a year, just by betting on horses. Today, that's more than $300,000 a year. "I don't bet anything now," Hill told Tennessee senator Estes Kefauver, chairman of the committee investigating organized crime. "I am afraid I will win, and then they will say I made more money than I did." As with everything in Virginia's life, the hearing got off to a rocky start, hit a peak and ended in disaster.

Hill's rapid-fire rejoinders to committee questions drew laughter and applause. She complained of the flash photography as soon as the hearing began. "Make them quit doing that," Hill barked at the senators. The senators quickly urged the press to knock it off, even though they told her other witnesses were subjected to the same treatment. "Most of them never went through with those bums what I did," Hill told the reporters.

When asked how the men who showered her with jewels and cash made their money, Hill said she "didn't know anything about anybody." Long after Virginia testified, she was subjected to sexist columns that described her figure and outfit and their effects on the senators and the senators'

Virginia Hill smiles for the camera in this publicity photograph. *Courtesy of the Associated Press.*

supposedly jealous wives. Retail sales dropped during the hearings, even as Easter neared, while people followed the spectacle at home or in bars. "The housewife's dilemma is, of course, cooking vs. crime," said the Associated Press (AP). They reported that women were glued to their television sets, including thirty-five thousand Brooklyn Red Cross volunteers who stayed home. Kefauver urged them to "get back on the job." He also read into the record a letter from a husband who was grateful that the hearings had kept his wife out of stores. That got some laughs.

Virginia Hill left the hearing not knowing that she had just become the celebrity she had always dreamed of being. Relentlessly trailed by reporters, Hill refused to answer the questions of male journalists. One of the men pointed to writer Marjorie Farnsworth of the *New York Journal-American* and asked, "Will you talk to this nice gal?" Virginia turned her angry gaze on Farnsworth. "You're just a dirty little bum." Hill then punched Farnsworth in the jaw. Unlike the other victims of Virginia's assaults, Farnsworth didn't require medical attention. As she made her way to a cab, Hill cursed at the reporters. "I hope the atom bomb falls on every one of you!" As Virginia pushed through the crowd, she alternately hid her face and snarled at cameras, kicked at a photographer and reared her hand back to strike another. Moments later, Virginia adjusted her large black velvet hat, smiled and posed for those very same photographers.

If a life can be encapsulated within the events of a single day, Hill's 1951 appearance in Washington, D.C. was pitch perfect—glamorous, brutal, cunning and charming. Virginia Hill had made herself a national star and an American villain in a matter of minutes. All of it would haunt her for the rest of her short life. The origins of that life have been told in many ways. She is frequently said to have been born in my hometown, Bessemer, in 1916. News reports also listed her place of birth as Marietta, Georgia; Ellis Island; and even Holland.

A descendant of Hill's tells me she was from Lipscomb, Alabama, the birthplace the Internal Revenue Service listed on her wanted poster when they pursued her for unpaid taxes. That poster said Virginia used twenty-two aliases and was "a paramour and associate of racketeers and gangsters."

Her life story has been told in books, television and movies, most notably, when Virginia was portrayed by actress Annette Bening, opposite Warren Beatty as Siegel, in 1991's *Bugsy*. It was on the set of that movie that the two screen legends began their decades-long love affair. "[Hill] was volatile and foul-mouthed but also big-hearted and lots of fun," Bening said in a 1992 *Washington Post* interview.

It all began on an Alabama horse farm on August 26, 1916. The family later moved to Marietta, although Hill was often referred to as "an Alabama heiress." Her family was, at best, middle class. Legendary TV host Ed Sullivan wrote in his "Little Old New York" column in 1947, "AP still refers to Virginia Hill as an 'heiress?' Are they kidding?"

The life of the young "Alabama heiress" was far from easy. Sick of the brutal beatings she, her siblings and her mother endured from her drunken, tombstone polisher father, Hill, at age seven, burned him with boiling grease. Virginia was always willing to use violence to protect herself and those she loved, earning her the nickname "Tabby" because she fought like a wildcat.

Virginia Hill "claws at news photographers as she enters an elevator in the swank Ambassador East Hotel in Chicago, March 9, 1950." *Courtesy of the Associated Press.*

What drew people to Virginia was her charm, biting wit and thirst for life—something one can only understand if they grew up poor in the South. "When she was young, Virginia talked about being a movie star, and she always brought people home and cooked for them and entertained them," Hill's sister B.H. Ward once said. By the time she was a teenager, Virginia was looking for some way to escape. "Because she had very little education, she looked for a way out of poverty. She started out working at horse tracks," I was told by Gary Pullen, a south Alabama man whose grandmother was Virginia's baby sister and whose mother was named after Virginia. "That's where she met up with the mobsters who liked her looks and spunk. She moved up from there in a very short time. I think many in her family admired that about her."

"A TOUGH AND CUNNING FIGHTER"

By the time she was fifteen, Virginia had fled to Chicago and found herself immersed in the blood-soaked world of some of history's most notorious criminals. Her father sent the police out to bring her home, but she managed to elude them. "She began working as a waitress and prostitute. Joe Epstein, a bookie for [Al] Capone, is said to have called her the Flamingo because of her long legs," journalist Paul Byrnes wrote.

Years later, the nickname Flamingo followed Hill to the Las Vegas casino that might very well have led to Siegel's death. Epstein, who for years managed Hill's money, vanished after Hill's Senate testimony spawned headlines calling him "Virginia's Santa Claus." In the 1930s, Virginia served as a "bag woman" for many other powerful figures in organized crime, carrying the syndicate's cash from city to city. "Virginia Hill was a tough and cunning woman, a fighter, a master at timing who knew how to seize an opportunity to her advantage," Andy Edmonds wrote in her 1993 book *Bugsy's Baby: The Secret Life of Mob Queen Virginia Hill.*

"It was common knowledge in both the Mafia and law enforcement that Hill had in her possession the tools to destroy the East Coast mob and send the Chicago outfit tumbling like a house of cards." As she gathered an arsenal of underworld blackmail material, Virginia married four times in nineteen years. In 1931, at the age of fifteen, she married a fellow teen named George Randall. They divorced in 1934, when she was about eighteen. In 1939, she married University of Alabama football player Ossie Griffith in a drunken stupor—they split after less than a year. A year after Hill divorced Griffith, she married Mexican rumba dancer Carlos Gonzales; they divorced in 1944. Her fourth and final husband was Hans Hauser, a German-Austrian ski instructor she married in 1950.

Hill also built a fortune her family couldn't have dreamed of. In 1941, Virginia threw a $7,500 party at the Hollywood club Mocambo. Two years later, she bought a New York nightclub, Hurricane, for $60,000 in cash. After Epstein warned her of possible tax troubles, she gave the club to her employees, saying it was "a gift from Virginia." Hill's brother Charles once watched her pay $6,400 in cash for a 1947 Cadillac. "Just a few weeks ago, she gave a champagne party in Hollywood for 20 guests, and I don't know where she got the dough to pay for it," he told a reporter. "I've never tried to figure out where it comes from. It's none of my affair," said Charles, who was nicknamed Chick.

At some point, Virginia met the infamous outlaw with whom she would share a tumultuous, tragic love affair that read like a Shakespearean play. Accounts of her first meeting with Siegel vary, saying it took place sometime between 1937 and 1943. Either way, the volatile relationship ended with Bugsy dead on her couch in 1947, shot multiple times with a newspaper in his hand.

"SHE'S NOBODY TO FOOL WITH"

Born in 1906, Siegel is remembered by his "Bugsy" nickname, which he hated but had earned with his wild temperament. Along with Meyer Lansky, Charles "Lucky" Luciano and Arnold Rothstein, Bugsy helped forge one of the most notorious New York crime outfits of the Prohibition era. Siegel and Hill met in New York while she was ferrying gangster cash, and they continued their affair at the Hollywood home of famous actor George Raft, one of Siegel's pals from his Hell's Kitchen childhood.

Hill was in Los Angeles, pursuing her childhood dream of stardom, achieving only a bit part as a hat check girl in 1941's *Manpower*, but she enjoyed hobnobbing with stars. "In Hollywood, in Rudolph Valentino's old mansion, mother said Virginia would bring in movie stars at 3 and 4 in the morning and cook for them," Virginia's sister, B.H. Ward, would later recall. Hill, Ward said, could have been a movie star herself, as she barely lost out on a role to Jean Harlow in *Hell's Angels*.

Benjamin "Bugsy" Siegel shown in a 1928 mugshot. *Courtesy of the New York Police Department.*

Siegel was presumably in Los Angeles on gangland business. Although he was married and had two daughters, he and Hill engaged in voracious lovemaking and vicious fights that brought the cops. "Most every other man she knew she'd been able to dominate," Bening said in 1992. "She really wanted to dominate him as well, but the fact that she couldn't was a real turn-on. She was a woman with a lot of guts. She knew how to talk and stand up to men. She had a mind of her own. She was very liberated, had lots of relationships. But when she met Ben, she really fell in love and wanted to be with him only."

Siegel's status in the underworld plummeted when he decided to build the Flamingo Hotel and Casino, named in honor of Virginia's long legs, in the middle of the Las Vegas desert. The skyrocketing cost of the Flamingo was bringing Siegel unwanted attention. Hill spent little time at the Flamingo because of her allergies, but apparently, she visited often enough to grow bitterly jealous of Marie "The Body" McDonald, a model who was a guest there. Bugsy's bodyguards were on alert to protect Marie from Virginia.

When Marie left, Virginia's rage-filled attention turned to Betty Dexter, a former model who ran the Flamingo's coat check and magazine stands and who oversaw the cigarette girls. Virginia tried, unsuccessfully, to have Betty fired, fearing she was catching Bugsy's eye. One night, while Hill was drinking heavily at the Flamingo, her red-hot anger became focused on Betty. "Suddenly, she went berserk," the *New York Daily News* reported. Virginia attacked Betty, and the two fought for more than a minute, rolling on the carpet in the middle of the casino as more than one hundred patrons and partygoers looked on in horror. Virginia had the upper hand when card dealer Larry Stein pulled her off of Betty. The *Daily News* reported, "He carried her out, biting and kicking, and locked her inside the hotel office, where Siegel had been working with no knowledge of the brawl outside. Immediately, Virginia turned her wrath on him." Those outside the office heard Virginia shouting accusations. The *Daily News* article continued, "Then they heard something else: the smack of Bugsy's open hand as he slapped her into submission. Later, when she took off, she refused to see him." Betty was taken to the hospital with a dislocated vertebra. "She's nobody to fool with," Betty later said of Virginia, whom she sued. Virginia avoided Las Vegas until the statute of limitations on that suit expired.

Virginia calmly explained the episode to senators four years later. "I hit a girl at the Flamingo, and [Siegel] told me I wasn't a lady. We got in a big fight. I had been drinking, and I left, and I went to Paris." Not long after Virginia left for France, Siegel pulled out the golden key that had been specially made for him and entered Hill's Beverly Hills mansion. Upstairs were Hill's brother Chick and her secretary, Jerri Mason. Siegel was reading the *Los Angeles Times* while sitting on the couch with business associate Allen Smiley when nine shots rang out from a .30-caliber rifle. Two rounds hit Siegel in the chest and another two hit him in the head. It was 10:45 p.m. on June 20, 1947. Bugsy Siegel was dead at the age of forty-one. The murder has never been solved.

Virginia, at the time, was sailing on a houseboat in France. She had also been frequenting nightclubs, gazing out of the window of her hotel room in Paris's Rue de la Paix district and was at a party two days after the shooting. "We got to talking calisthenics, and I told another American girl: 'I know a fellow who loves calisthenics and does them very well—Ben Siegel,'" the International News Service (INS) quoted Virginia as saying. "She looked at me strangely and replied: 'Why, he's dead. Didn't you know?' That was the first I had heard about it….It looks so bad to have a thing like that happen there."

Thus began a downward spiral for thirty-year-old Virginia Hill.

"THE MOST GOSSIPED-ABOUT NATIVE OF ALABAMA"

Journalists flocked to Virginia in Paris, desperate for the sordid details of her affair with Bugsy. "He was one of the finest men I ever met, and he had the greatest respect for me," Hill told them. "He had a terrific temper. He would jump down people's throats and shout at me in front of other people." Reporters also asked about his life of crime. "Ben was no dope peddler. He was just a good gambler, and what is wrong with that?" They wanted to know if she had any theories as to who gunned down Bugsy. "My God, nothing like this has ever happened to me before. I heard about this last night, and it's made me sick." The AP reported that Hill "almost shrieked to reporters" and refused their requests to see her. "I'm sick. I'm feverish. I don't want to see anybody."

One theory held that Hill had recently taken up with another man who jealously hired gunmen to kill Siegel. Another was that she killed him out of jealousy over a woman he was seeing. There were many theories but few facts. "There might have been a hundred different people who wanted Siegel out of the way. There were plenty who had motive enough to kill him," Chief Deputy D.A. Ernest Roll told reporters. "I can't imagine who shot him or why," Hill told the United Press. "There was no mistress business involved. If anyone or anything was his mistress, it was that Las Vegas hotel. He was killing himself putting it into shape."

A few days after Hill learned of the murder, a reporter tried to show her a picture of Bugsy's blood-drenched corpse. She tried to steer the conversation to the green satin nightgown with silver trimming she was wearing to a ball that night. "I've got a date for lunch, and I'd better go. Take that awful picture of Ben out of here. I don't want to spoil my vacation."

Newspaper reporters were obsessed with the woman they called the "most gossiped-about native of Alabama." They weren't alone. A week after Siegel's murder, California attorney general Fred Howser cabled Paris authorities to get a statement from Hill. It was rumored that hitmen were on their way to France to keep Virginia quiet. Lawmen in the United States feared if they didn't kill Virginia in Europe, they would get her as soon as she returned to America. Pullen told me:

> My mom always told us when growing up that when she was young, she remembered several suspected members of the mob snooping around their house in Chickasaw, Alabama, looking for signs of Virginia Hill. They saw some type of machine gun in one of their hands. They knew for several years that their house was being watched.

If gunmen were out to get Hill, they weren't trying as hard as she was to kill herself. In a matter of weeks in the summer of 1947, Hill nearly died multiple times in Paris hospitals as she swallowed handfuls of sleeping pills. Publicist David Green said a "scion of a wealthy French business family," whom Hill had been spending time with, saw newspapers piled up outside her door and kicked it in. Hill woke up furious in a hospital bed. "She tore up her passport and flushed it down the drain. She threw vases and dishes at everybody around and accused the young nobleman of stealing her jewels—which he had considerately placed in the hotel safe," INS reported.

While recovering with a glass of cognac by the pool of the Hotel La Reserve, Hill told a reporter that, although she was "worried and nervous," her most recent overdose had been an accident. "I'm hiding from sorrow, not fear. There are no gangsters on my track. Ben wasn't a gangster, either. I took the tablets so I could sleep. I took too many, I guess. All I want is to be left alone with my sorrows. What I seek most is solitude," she said as she refilled her drink. "I am afraid of nothing. If someone wishes to kill me, he doesn't have to come to Europe to do it. They can expect me in the United States shortly. I have nothing to hide.…I am nothing but a dizzy girl. No man in the world, least of all Siegel, would have entrusted any important documents to me." However, locksmith William E. Morin, who made Bugsy's golden key, told reporters that he was often called to the mansion to change the combination to a safe when the two fought.

Less than a month after Bugsy's murder, hundreds of people who gathered at New York's LaGuardia Airport were disappointed when news of her return to America proved to be untrue. She was, however, preparing to return to the United States. "I'll probably go to Alabama—that used to be my home. It was long ago that I had a family and anybody cared what happened to me. But I probably won't get there, ever. I'll probably jump out of the plane first."

"I Don't Care to Live"

As Hill threatened another suicide attempt, Chick saw to it that a Miami Beach mansion was equipped with floodlights, armed guards and alarms linked to the local police department to keep anyone else from taking her life. The house on Sunset Island No. 1 had been purchased from the son of publisher William Randolph Hearst, possibly with Bugsy's money.

Miami Beach police were also preparing for her arrival and for any hitmen who might have been preparing their own welcome home for Virginia. "I think some gangsters are on Miami Beach just waiting for the opportunity to kill Miss Hill," Miami Beach police chief P.R. Short told reporters.

Journalists waited as Hill boarded a plane in Paris in August 1947. "I'll knock your block off," she yelled as she took a clumsy swing at journalist Dorothy Russell. Hill then sobbed, "I don't want to be mean to you....Now that they've killed Ben, I am completely alone in the world. I have no home, and life isn't worth living." As she crossed the Atlantic Ocean, reporters and police guards were waiting for her plane to land. When she arrived, Hill wasn't eager to talk. "I have nothing to say. Don't you understand English? I'll never grant another interview or talk with anyone from the press. They've been making up stories about me for eight weeks. Even if they cut my tongue out, I won't talk to them." Although she said she could take care of herself, Hill made it clear she had no desire to keep on living. "I don't care to live in a world where people go around saying all the mean things they can about someone else."

A few weeks after arriving at her fortified Miami Beach mansion, Hill came out of a sixty-seven-hour self-induced sleeping pill coma. She had been found unconscious with a picture of Bugsy resting under her head. It wasn't immediately certain whether Hill would survive this suicide attempt. When she awoke, Miami Beach police were eager to chat with Virginia. "If you are going to get killed, go to California and get killed," Short said he had told her. "The showdown is coming. We told Virginia once to lay off the sleeping pills, and to get out of the state if she was going to get killed. We told her that we thought the same gangsters who killed Bugsy would like to get her," Detective Chief Charles W. Pierce said.

Hill didn't stay where she wasn't wanted. After recovering, she left Miami Beach; her guards were dismissed, and the home's elaborate security system was dismantled. "Friends of Virginia Hill, intimate of the late Bugsy Siegel, insist she will continue with her suicide attempts until she succeeds or—what is even worse—the papers stop mentioning it," journalist Leonard Lyons wrote in his column, "The Lyons Den," on August 28, 1947. It was said she went to Mexico, where she spent 23,000 pesos in a nightclub in a single night and $11,000 in U.S. currency in six weeks.

Less than four months after Virginia fled Florida, a woman was admitted to Phoenix's Good Samaritan Hospital under the name Norma Hall of Chicago. She had overdosed on sleeping powders at the Paradise Inn, where she had been staying since November 24. When she awoke, she threatened to sue police if they entered her hospital room, and she gave a nurse $1,200 in cash that was to be put in a hospital safe. Officers used a photograph to determine that Norma Hall was Virginia Hill. It was her fourth suicide attempt in five months. While sedated, Hill said that "gangsters" were after her and that she intended to "beat them to it" by killing herself.

"We know there's an increasing influx of gangsters here, and we want to know who they are and what they intend to do. We want to run them out," Phoenix police chief Earl O'Clair told reporters. Two men who Chief O'Clair said were Hill's bodyguards entered her room late one night. "They told a supervisor that a good friend of the patient had been killed recently and that she was in a highly nervous state. They frightened the nurses by saying the 'Chicago underworld' was after her," the AP reported.

The many articles about Virginia after Bugsy's murder frequently described her as an "auburn-haired beauty," "shapely" or as a "dark-haired girlfriend," visualizations that caught the eye of Lucy O'Brien, who wrote the *Tampa Tribune*'s "Woman's World" column and was the paper's first female reporter.

> *Have you ever noticed how gangster's molls, murderesses and women who meet sudden or violent deaths are almost always reported as being something special to look at?...Pretty, vivacious and attractive are adjectives popularly applied to these newsworthy ladies. There must be some immutable law which requires females of the species who are more deadly than the male to be extra-specially glamorous....Her looks are always worth comment.*

America's fascination with Virginia Hill waned as 1947 came to an end, but it was renewed with a fury in 1951, when the U.S. Senate put the Alabama mob queen on display for twenty-one million American television viewers across the country.

"AN ASTOUNDING PERFORMANCE OF VULGAR IMPUDENCE"

Virginia had dreamed of being famous since she was a child. In 1951, her dream came true but at a Senate hearing instead of a Hollywood premiere. Though she carefully guarded the secrets of the gangsters she had befriended and bedded over twenty years, Virginia's testimony sent the federal government after her like a bloodhound. In a matter of minutes, her words turned her into a celebrity, a pariah, a legend and a fugitive.

"The life of Virginia Hill sounds glamorous to the uninitiated," the venerable journalist Walter Winchell wrote after her testimony. "For every girl like Virginia Hill, who hit the highlights of the Shadow Circuit, there are 10,000 pitifully dependent upon the whim of a criminal's twisted mind for their next meal."

Scripps-Howard columnist and big-game hunter Robert C. Ruark wrote, "She appeared to have the entire committee mesmerized, as a bird stares hopefully at a snake. You even believed that Virginia Hill exists, which, of course, cannot possibly be true. She is a mirage, thought up by a drunken magician." He added that Hill's testimony had "created a new art form." He continued, "Virginia Hill seems to have been an Alice in a wonderland of illegality....Any secrets she holds are safe because this is a girl who don't know nothin' about nobody and is little loath to say so."

"Senator Kefauver noted with some alarm that some segments of the populace showed a tendency to sympathize with the witnesses, no matter how shady their past," wrote columnist John Crosby, who was then one of the nation's leading TV critics. "The one person who seems to have won universal acclaim after a stint before the cameras was Virginia Hill, which suggests this isn't so Puritan a country after all."

Columnist George Sokolsky wrote, "Where did she get all the money she spent? From the men she went out with....We used to have a name for that and those who pursued such a vocation were not encouraged to mingle with other folks....It was an astounding performance of vulgar impudence."

Having testified to receiving gifts from gangsters and more gambling winnings than she could count, the IRS and FBI were quickly on Virginia's trail, as she was indicted by a federal grand jury on charges of tax evasion. They put her on the "Most Wanted" list, printing up wanted posters, just as they had for her gangland acquaintances decades earlier. She had fled to Austria by the time the government auctioned her property to pay back taxes.

For several years in the 1950s, Hill was a jetsetter, traveling all over Europe and beyond. By the 1960s, Virginia was out of money and had yet again lost her will to live. Virginia once offered the IRS $100,000 just to return to the United States, according to her sister, B.H. Ward. "They said it wasn't enough. Virginia just wanted to come back and see our mother before she died....She kept my mother up like a queen with diamonds and clothes."

Virginia Hill testifies at a U.S. Senate hearing on organized crime in 1951. *Courtesy of the Associated Press.*

Separated from her husband, Hill lived with her fifteen-year-old son, Peter Hauser, and took to walking the mountains in high heels until she grew tired of the attention. "The hell with this stuff. All these jerks watch me like I was on exhibition," she told a reporter. In 1965, she survived her seventh suicide attempt. Her son supported her by working as a waiter, and they lived in an Alpine hut, where she wrote her memoirs, despite her fear of revenge from the gangsters she planned to mention in the book. She kept a gun handy in case of unexpected visitors. Hill never finished the book.

Virginia Hill left home on March 22, 1965, some say to meet her old lover, Genovese crime boss Joe Adonis. Her lifeless body was found two days later in the snow, alongside a tree-shaded brook near a nightclub just outside Salzburg. She was found five thousand miles from where her life had begun just forty-nine years earlier. "Her coat was neatly folded on the ground. A possible suicide note indicated the person was simply 'tired of life,'" the Mob Museum wrote.

Of course, there is speculation that the mob finally silenced Virginia Hill for good, before she could tell her own unbelievable life story. "I can't understand why my mother died so suddenly and under mysterious circumstances," Peter told reporters. "Virginia was real nice to all of us, and we knew she was a good girl. She put all of our brothers in business and put Charles, the youngest one, through college in California," her sister, B.H. Ward, told the *Huntsville Times*. "If she ever knew anybody in the underworld, we didn't know about it," Ward said. "Virginia could have been a movie star, too. They offered her some of Jean Harlow's parts, and she dyed her hair blonde after she went through the Pasadena Play House, but she just didn't have time....Virginia never had any girls to play with, only her three younger brothers, so I guess that's why she turned out to be a tomboy."

Hill's legacy lives on in everything from the hard-to-find copy of the 1974 made-for-TV biopic starring Dyan Cannon and Harvey Keitel to the Pensacola car dealership bearing her last name. Virginia's family carries her legacy in the many stories and jewels she left behind. Some of her descendants turned to the church, chastened by her tragic life, while others tried their damnedest to recreate it. "My mom witnessed so much alcoholism and abuse that it turned her against that lifestyle. She raised us in church. Unfortunately, I think the majority of the family was proud of the fact that we were kin to someone a little famous," Pullen said.

4

THE PUZZLING CASES OF ALABAMA'S FOUR 1950s POISONERS

As the Medical Association of Alabama's 1956 meeting ended in Birmingham, a young physician from Mobile made a strange request of the doctors from around the state. Dr. Henry Gewin said that when a patient's symptoms could not be explained or a cause of death could not be found, doctors should test the living for poison and demand autopsies for the dead.

Throughout the age of Eisenhower and Elvis, Alabama doctors had been baffled when otherwise healthy people—some members of the same family—suddenly became violently ill, sometimes to the point of paralysis or agonizing, unexplainable death. The culprit, in many cases, was arsenic—cheap, readily available and highly lethal—slipped into the food and drinks of doomed patients by the women closest to them.

"It is understandable that a physician who devotes his life to relief of suffering should find it hard to conceive anyone's deliberately causing suffering and death," Dr. Gewin said. "Yet, realism demands that the physician consider this possibility in all puzzling cases." Back home, in Mobile, Dr. Gewin had just seen such a tragedy unfold. A waitress there had recently been accused of fatally poisoning six family members over a span of twenty years. "Several different physicians signed death certificates for various members of this family without suspecting something other than natural causes was responsible for the patient's demise," Dr. Gewin said. The waitress was one of at least four Alabama women convicted of multiple poisoning deaths in the 1950s. One of the poisoners may have inspired a deadly successor in the 1970s, sparking one of the strangest crime sagas in Alabama history.

These women's penchant for poison filled many graves and forced Alabama to examine when autopsies were performed, how life insurance policies were issued and when inmates should be shown mercy or sent to their death. What was the reason for this murderous 1950s trend? Why were some women adding arsenic to their husband's whiskeys or their children's milk? Well, it was cheap, easy and could be lucrative, and it was possible to get away with it—many, many times.

"Women abhor violence, especially women in the middle and upper classes. Women are supposed to be the gentler, subordinate sex—the housewife and mother—and they will invariably choose a quiet, non-violent way to commit murder," criminologist Dr. Dudley Degroot said in a 1958 *UPI* article about poisonings in the South.

A three-ounce bottle of arsenic in those days cost twenty-nine cents and could kill thirty adults, the *Alabama Journal* reported in 1956. "Start off with a few drops in their coffee, whiskey or milk once a day for a week or so. Add a few drops daily and then let them go without. No sudden or dramatic deaths that way; fewer nosy physicians; with luck, no autopsies. The slow way is the neat way. The bones degenerate; the blood-forming organisms are halted."

Today, in Alabama, if you die while not actively being treated by a physician, it is very likely an autopsy will be performed. In the 1950s, a poisoning could have been chalked up to one of the thousands of maladies that ended lives too soon with little or no examination of the corpse. The increased use of autopsies in Alabama arose, in part, due to the gruesome legacy of these four female poisoners.

Unlike today, Alabama in the 1950s did not require insurance agents to have permission from individuals when insurance policies were purchased on their lives. One Selma poisoner was said to have held life insurance policies on 150 people without any of them knowing. Some of those policies paid off several thousand dollars.

For the victims, it was a tortuous demise, delivered by someone they may have trusted more than anyone else.

EARLE DENNISON

Shirley Dianne Weldon climbed onto Earle Dennison's lap on May 1, 1952, and hugged her neck, the child's face beaming with gratitude for the orange

Child poisoner Earle Dennison is led to jail in 1952. *Courtesy of the* Birmingham News.

soda her aunt had poured her. Hours later, the two-and-a-half-year-old with blue eyes and blonde, curly hair was dead after a sudden, violent illness.

Earle had gone to visit Cora Belle Weldon, the sister of her husband, Lemuel Dennison, who had died six months earlier at their farmhouse in rural Elmore County. Cora Belle and her husband, Gaston, had suffered tragedy themselves—their three-year-old daughter, Polly Ann, had died suddenly in 1949, not long after Shirley was born. Polly Ann began vomiting and was hospitalized after Earle gave the child an ice cream cone.

Nearly three years after that heartbreaking death, Earle went out to buy sodas for the family, dropping and breaking one. As Cora Belle cleaned up the mess, Earle divided the remaining drinks among the family, putting Shirley's in a formula cup. The child almost instantly began vomiting. "I suggested we should take her to the doctor. But Earle said no because the vomiting was just an upset stomach," Cora Belle later said. "My wife kept insisting on going to the doctor. She kept saying it was no use," Gaston would say.

The parents eventually insisted, and Earle went with the family to a doctor and then to Wetumpka General Hospital, where she worked as an operating room nurse, although she had not been licensed in the state for twenty years. Along the way, they stopped at a store. "[Earle] was carrying little Shirley and patted the child on the head saying, 'Bless your little heart,'" a store employee later said. Earle didn't stay at the hospital for very long after dropping off Shirley. Dr. G.L. Gresham rebuked Earle for not getting the child there sooner and for not telling them that she had been treated by another doctor.

Earle went straight from the hospital to the home of insurance agent Cecil Bailey to pay the overdue premium on a life insurance policy on Shirley—it would have lapsed the next day. The child died at 8:15 p.m. Earle returned after the child's death and reacted with indifference when she heard the news, hospital employees testified. "All she had to say was, 'Aw,'" one employee said. "She said it didn't look like it hurt her much," Alma Hall testified. Although Earle seemed to care little about Shirley when she was sick, funeral home employee John Edward Ward said she watched the autopsy with great interest, asked why it was being done and rubbed her hands nervously.

One week after Shirley's death, as Elmore County sheriff Lester Holley closed in on her, Earle attempted to take her life with an overdose of pills. "She took something that knocked her out. I took her to the hospital, and they fixed her up," Holley said. "It is a terrible thing, and nobody knows what it's like who hasn't suffered through this," Cora Belle said of Shirley's death.

Dennison reads while
incarcerated in 1953. *Courtesy of
the* Birmingham News.

While recovering from that suicide attempt, Earle confessed to killing Shirley but denied murdering Polly Ann Weldon. "It didn't cross my mind that they could go into the body and find out if the child was poisoned with arsenic. I wouldn't have given it arsenic if I thought they could find it," Earle said during her confession to Shirley's murder.

Earle said that around the time Polly Ann got sick, she accidentally brought an eighth of an ounce of arsenic in a saltshaker to their home and left it there. She had brought food to the family while Cora Belle was in the hospital with newborn Shirley. Earle said she kept the poison in the shaker to kill ants at her home. The family didn't use it, and when Earle returned the next day, she gave Polly Ann ice cream. Although Earle denied it was poisoned, half an hour later, Polly Ann went into convulsions and died about four days later at the hospital where Earle worked and where Shirley was born. Earle stayed with Polly Ann, even in her off hours. At the time, she had a $5,000 life insurance policy on Polly Ann and the child's seven-year-old brother, Orvil. Earle had another $5,500 policy on Shirley but wouldn't discuss the motive for her murder. "She just shut up and wouldn't talk whenever we tried to bring up the subject," Holley said.

Dennison in the Jefferson County Jail in August 1952, awaiting the outcome of her appeal from a death sentence imposed by a jury. With her are Chief Deputy Wilton Hogan, Highway Patrolman Ed Owen and Kilby Matron Vera Vinson. *Courtesy of the* Birmingham News.

Earle's trial in August 1952 drew two thousand spectators who were disappointed when the proceedings were delayed for twenty-four hours after Earle again tried to take her own life. With a guard sitting nearby, she hid both of her hands under a blanket at Tutwiler Prison and sawed at her wrist with a jagged piece of razor she had found in the trash. She called for a prison nurse at 5:45 a.m., saying she wasn't feeling well. The nurse peeled back the blanket to discover her blood-soaked mattress; Earle had lost a pint or more of blood and needed a transfusion. "I'm sorry. I must have been out of my mind," Earle told prison employees. She left a note with a list of names and asked that the hymns "Old Rugged Cross" and "Rock of Ages" be sung at her funeral. "My people did not know anything about this," she wrote at the bottom.

As Earle recovered, the body of Lemuel Dennison was exhumed. No arsenic was found. At her trial, defense attorney W.C. Woodall objected to the use of the confessions, saying that the statements were made when Earle was in a "weakened" state. Testimony revealed that Earle's husband had been an institutionalized alcoholic, which may have led to her unhappy home life. Her brother-in-law James Crowell said she borrowed money from him "at least 100 times." Earle's sister Sula Crowell said that she "was not the sister I used to know," and Dr. J.S. Harmon said that, although he treated Earle for nervousness, "most women her age" are nervous. Her family said that since the death of her husband, Lemuel, in October 1951, she had acted strangely, grieving hour after hour at her husband's grave.

At 9:25 p.m. on Saturday August 16, 1952, an all-male jury—women were not allowed to serve on Alabama juries until 1966—convicted Earle Dennison. She was sentenced to death.

As 1953 began, Earle hoped for mercy from the Alabama Supreme Court; she read several chapters of the Bible a day and cleaned the prison matron's apartment. When asked by the *Montgomery Advertiser* if she did any cooking, Earle replied with a sob, "I've forgotten how. I couldn't cook now." On September 1, 1953, Earle was placed in Kilby's death cell, and she was watched at all hours in case of another suicide attempt. As her date with death neared, Earle shrunk from 131 pounds to 100 and said she didn't "remember much about the case." She said her death sentence was "too much….It wasn't fair." When shuttled to psychiatric examinations and clemency hearings, Earle was repeatedly stripped naked to prevent another suicide attempt. A woman stayed in her cell around the clock, and an armed guard remained outside the barred door.

Dennison shown on the day of her September 4, 1953 execution. *Courtesy of the Birmingham News.*

Governor Gordon Persons, however, refused to spare her life, and he said she was to die at midnight on September 4, 1953. She had begged him, "Have mercy on me. Spare my life." Earle had hoped the governor would commute her sentence to life imprisonment so she could "work with other women and girls to help them lead a better life." She had led Sunday services and fainted when she learned that her appeal had been denied. The prison matron roused her with ammonia. "I could devote my life to helping others and redeem myself," she said. "There is no doubt in my mind of Mrs. Dennison's guilt. May God rest Mrs. Dennison's soul," Persons said. The fact that she was a White woman made no difference, he said. The only other woman to die in the state's electric chair, up to that point, was Silena Gilmore, who was Black. "The child is just as dead as if the crime had been committed by a man," Persons said.

The *Birmingham News* reported that, on "a clear and starry night," her head was shaved at 10:00 p.m., and an undertaker was arranging her funeral. At 5:00 p.m., she had a "beautiful dinner" of fried chicken, asparagus tips, tossed salad, mashed potatoes, ice cream and coffee with cream. She ate it all and was given a mild sedative at 7:30 p.m. "to kind of calm her." "She said she held no grudge or animosity against anyone. She said her heart is clean," said prison chaplain J.E. Franks. "With a simple prayer of forgiveness on her quivering lips, Mrs. Earle Dennison paid with her life early today," the *Alabama Journal* reported. "God has forgiven me for all I have done. Please forgive me for what I did. I forgive everyone," Earle said.

She was led into the green execution chamber of Kilby Prison at 12:02 a.m., and she was strapped into the Big Yellow Mama. "Her head shaven and her nose slightly red from an apparent crying spell, she seemed prepared to accept her fate with complete resignation," the *Alabama Journal* reported.

Three guards took four minutes to adjust the ten straps, including a halo-like leather band that was soaked in a saltwater solution. Her horn-rimmed glasses were removed, and a black hood was placed over her head. An attendant waved a yellow paddle to the executioner, who was in another room. She was hit with 2,600 volts for twenty-seven seconds starting at 12:07 a.m., as fifteen reporters watched from four feet away. The current entered her left leg, and her body tensed. The electricity pouring through her body made a "gurgling sound," and when it was over, the smell of "burning feathers" filled the room.

A doctor then tore open her dress and placed a stethoscope on her chest, leaving a small, white circle above her bra line. She was pronounced dead at 12:12 a.m. "I feel nothing but sorrow for Mrs. Dennison, but at the same time, I have to remember she did not show any mercy to my little girl," Shirley's father said.

Dozens of sleepy prisoners gawked as her body was carried out through the prison yard. Near the gate, she was covered in a blue velvet cloth, and a hearse drove her away at 12:19 a.m. Earle Dennison was buried at 5:00 a.m. in a small ceremony with her relatives at Pierce's Chapel, near Holtsville.

"GIGGLING GRANNY" NANNIE DOSS

Nannie Doss laughed a number of times during her twenty-four-hour interrogation with Tulsa investigators in November 1954. In the interrogation, she rattled off the details of her husbands' murders and apologized to weary detectives. "I feel awful bad about keeping you fellows up this way. I'm sorry to be so much trouble."

After the Alabama native confessed to poisoning four of her five husbands, police trotted her out for a televised interview, but they only allowed detectives to ask questions. "She insisted on prettying herself for the occasion. She smiled and seemed to enjoy herself during the brief

Nannie Doss gives photographers a smile after receiving a life sentence in June 1955 for the rat poison murder of her fifth husband, Samuel Doss, one of the four she admitted to disposing of by using rodent killer. *Courtesy of the Associated Press.*

questioning," AP reported on November 28, 1954. Thus, Nannie Doss became the Giggling Granny. She said her first victim was her second husband, Ernest Harrelson, in Jacksonville, Alabama, in 1945. She confessed to putting rat poison in his corn whisky because she claimed he mistreated her, but she denied killing his two-and-a-half-year-old grandson two months before Harrelson died. Nannie said Ernest beat her, so she poured the poison into his "rotgut" jug. She said he had tried to force her "to go to bed with him" after a bender and had said, "'If you don't go to bed with me now, I won't be here next week.' I decided, 'I'll teach him,' and I did." She and Harrelson were common law spouses, as they couldn't get a marriage license after Nannie's divorce from her first husband, Charlie Bragg of Alabama City.

Bragg and Doss were married in 1921 and divorced seven years later, after having four daughters and one son together. They divorced after he found out that she was running around with other men, INS reported. "She was a pretty girl, good build and lots of fun," Bragg said. Then she started running around. "About eight years of this was enough. I decided it was all off when she came home to our house with a man with her." Bragg said he wouldn't eat anything she cooked when she was mad, which was often. "She was no more Christian than if she had never heard the Bible preached. I told my mother that."

Of their five children, one died right after birth and two—Zelma and Gertrude—died in 1922, both around the age of two. Charlie said the neighbors told him that after he left, they were vomiting as if they had been poisoned. "I was scared to death and so were all my relatives. She was a peculiar woman who wouldn't sit still very long….Some of the neighbors said there was something funny about the way they died because they turned black so quick."

Doss soon met Harrelson. "He was an awful drunkard," she said, and after a night of drinking in 1945, he threatened to leave her if she wouldn't go to bed with him. "I got to thinking about what he said and thought, 'I'll just teach him.'" Despite poisoning him, Doss said she really loved Harrelson, even buying a grave plot and tombstone inscribed "Nannie Harrelson" to be buried next to him.

Then she married Harley Lanning of Lexington, North Carolina, in 1947. Doss was jealous because the laborer was "running around with other women" in 1952. Lanning died days after his food was poisoned. She supervised his funeral and had "God Be with You Until We Meet Again" inscribed on his tombstone. She said she was through with romance because "the Lord has already taken two of my husbands away."

Lanning's relatives told Lexington coroner David Plummer they suspected foul play. In April 1953, Plummer heard the same claim from another source and had Lanning's body exhumed. Doss later confessed, blaming Lanning's womanizing for her decision to murder him. "It brought on serious trouble, and then I put rat poison in his food," she explained.

Doss then joined the St. Louis Lonely Hearts Club and began corresponding with Richard Morton, sixty-four, of Emporia, Kansas. He was described as a "part-Indian" man from Oklahoma and was soon to be her fourth husband. About fourteen months after Lanning died, Morton wrote the head of the lonely hearts club, Floyd Finley, and asked that his and Nannie's names be removed from the rolls. "We have met and are happily married. She is a sweet and wonderful person." Four months later, she put rat poison in his coffee because "he was fixing to run around with another woman." Doss later said, "I lost my head and blew up when I found out he had been running around with another woman and had bought some rings." She poured an entire bottle of poison into a cup, filled the rest with coffee and gave it to Morton. He got sick on the job at a billiards parlor, went home and died the next day. "I think I've drunk too much coffee lately," he said before leaving the pool hall. His dog grew violently ill a few days later and died.

Doss was soon back on the lonely hearts listings and met husband number five, marrying Samuel Doss, fifty-eight, of Tulsa in June 1953. "He was mean," she explained, saying he wouldn't buy her an electric fan or television. "He was so religious he wouldn't let me watch television or have any magazines in the house and made me go to bed early.…He got on my nerves." She said she put rat poison in his coffee and prunes. "He sure did like prunes. I fixed a whole box, and he ate them all." Samuel, a highway

Doss is interviewed for KTVX by officers on November 28, 1954, in Tulsa, Oklahoma. Doss talked with police commissioner John Henderson, Captain Harry Stege and county attorney J. Howard Edmondson, who can be seen holding a signed statement in which Doss admitted to poisoning two husbands. *Courtesy of the Associated Press.*

employee who had lost his family to a tornado, spent most of October 1953 hospitalized. When he got out after twenty-three days, Nannie put a spoonful of poison in his coffee, and he died the next day in the hospital.

After she was caught, it was found Nannie was listed on the will for his $1,000 estate. She agreed to Samuel's autopsy after a doctor who couldn't find the cause of his death said he feared whatever killed him "might kill somebody else." A report by an Oklahoma Bureau of Investigation laboratory found that Samuel had enough poison in his system "to kill a horse."

While Samuel Doss was in the hospital, dairy farmer John H. Keel of Goldsboro, North Carolina, sixty, started corresponding with Nannie. She sent him a cake. Keel said he "had it in the back of [his] mind" that he might marry her. "I'm mighty proud she didn't come down here," he told INS.

After five of her husbands died in nine years, Nannie Doss caught the attention of police. They were suspicious of her growing list of dead husbands. While working as a housekeeper and babysitter to a couple in Tulsa, police picked her up on November 26, 1954. "Her jolly disposition never changed, as she denied knowing anything about the arsenic that killed Doss. Eight interrogators working in two-man teams questioned her for seven hours that night before she was permitted to go to bed. She joked and giggled through the entire session and admitted nothing," INS reported. The interrogation started at 10:00 a.m. and continued until she cracked at 10:00 p.m. "Yes, I killed him," she finally admitted. She signed a formal statement just before midnight.

During that marathon interrogation, Nannie's family in North Carolina and Alabama saw wire reports on the case in their local newspapers and contacted Tulsa police. One of her daughters with Braggs, Melvina Hedrick, asked that the body of her two-and-a-half-year-old son, Robert Lee Higgins, and Doss's mother, Dovie Weaver, be exhumed. She said something was "awfully funny" about her son's death. He had been staying with Nannie when he died. Both bodies had traces of poison but not a fatal amount. The death of Doss's sister, Sula Bartlett, in Gadsden in 1953 was also suddenly under scrutiny, as were the deaths of another grandchild and a woman Doss had cared for. Suspicion grew around the January 3, 1953 death of her seventy-four-year-old mother. She died a day before Doss left Lexington and met Morton.

Someone else who may have seen these reports back in Nannie's old Blue Mountain stomping grounds was twenty-one-year-old Audrey Marie Hilley, the subject of another chapter. Was she inspired by Nannie's murders twenty years later?

AP reported that Nannie stated, "I'd never poison anyone. I married those men because I loved them, not for money." After hours of questioning, she came clean one husband at a time. "I killed Doss, but my conscience is clear." Doss was then confronted with an autopsy showing that Morton was poisoned. "All right, I killed him, too, but now, my conscience is clear." This process was repeated with Harrelson and Lanning, but she swore that was all. "You can dig up all the other graves in the world, but you won't find anything else on me."

"She answers just about all of our questions in a straightforward manner," investigators told AP. "She laughs when something funny is said. She looks you straight in the eye when she tells you she poisoned this husband or that." Described by reporters as "buxom, cheerful," the only time Nannie showed

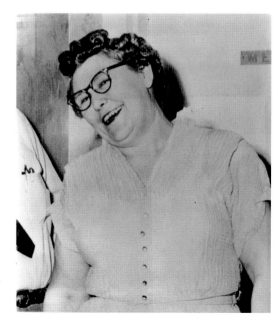

Nannie Doss gives photographers a smile after receiving a life sentence in June 1955 for the rat poison murder of her fifth husband, Samuel Doss, one of the four she admitted to disposing of by using rodent killer. *Courtesy of the Associated Press.*

any anger was when it was suggested that she killed her mother. "I loved my own mother more than my own life," she snapped. After being taken to a mental hospital for observation, Doss told a reporter that she was tricked into confessing but would likely go to prison for a long time. "They have so much evidence against me."

Nannie told the *Kansas City Times*, in November 1954, of her life growing up in Alabama, where she was born in Calhoun County in 1906, one of five children. She said her father left and came back only sporadically. Nannie said he was a "starter," meaning he'd plant a crop and leave before the harvest. She worked as a sharecropper with her mother to support the family. "I'd get down on my knees and crawl anywhere for my mother." Doss left school after fifth grade and started working in a Blue Mountain cotton mill at the age of fifteen. At some point, she suffered a massive head injury in a train accident and started thinking "crooked."

After one of her hearings, Nannie told a jail matron, "I don't understand those big legal words....Maybe those docs at the hospital will teach me to think straight." Prosecuted by future Oklahoma governor and U.S. senator James Howard Edmondson, Doss pleaded guilty and was given life in prison. "The day I entered, I told them to tell me what they wanted me to do and I would do it," Doss told the AP, months after being sent to prison on June 4, 1955. She worked in the prison laundry. "Did you notice I lost eight pounds since I have been down here? I do the washing the hard way."

Nannie had hoped that by pleading guilty, she would be sent to Eastern State Mental Hospital instead. She claimed the headaches she had suffered since her childhood injury were getting worse in prison. Later that year, she suffered a heart attack but recovered. "We get to go to movies, and we go to church and have television, and sometimes, we have dances."

On June 2, 1965, Nannie died in an Oklahoma City hospital at the age of sixty from leukemia. In reporting her death, the *UPI* called her "fat and 49" and said she had eleven victims in all. Doss went to her grave denying some of those murders. "I never harmed any of my blood kin."

RHONDA BELL MARTIN

Rhonda Bell Martin ended her shift at the Seabreeze Restaurant on Mobile's Concession Street on March 9, 1956, and made her way to her ten-dollar-a-week two-room apartment, still in her waitress uniform. State investigators

Rhonda Bell Martin lights a cigarette in June 1956. *Courtesy of the* Birmingham News.

pulled her into the back of a car. "I don't know why you are doing this. There's nothing to it," Martin reportedly proclaimed.

Montgomery Advertiser city editor Joe Azbell met with Rhonda in jail at 2:00 a.m. the following Saturday morning. Azbell published the earliest articles on the Montgomery bus boycott, interviewed and testified in defense of Martin Luther King Jr. and wrote speeches for Governor George Wallace. They talked for two hours as she wore wedding rings on both hands. Martin told Azbell that she had never dated a man she didn't marry. These men included fifty-one-year-old Claude Martin, who was poisoned to death in 1951, and even Claude's twenty-eight-year-old son, Ronald. Rhonda took up with Ronald, who was about twenty years younger than her, after his father's death. At the time of her arrest, the young man was suddenly fighting for his life at a VA hospital in Biloxi, Mississippi.

Rhonda said that when Claude died, she spent $400 of his insurance money to have his first wife's body moved to the plot next to his. "I knew Claude would have wanted that." Ronald, she said, "will be heartbroken when he finds out what happened to me." She said he recently bought her a sewing machine so she could quit waitressing. During a recent visit, she said he kissed her tenderly and told her he hated to see her go. "I love him so much....We've been so happy together." Rhonda continued:

Everybody always said I spoiled my husbands, and everybody always said I spoiled my children. That's the way I am. I always spoil anybody I love....If they say I poisoned anyone, they're wrong. I have never had a touch of poison in my hand in my life. There has never been any poison in my home in my life. I took care of Claude. Ronald and I gave him hypodermic shots when he was sick, and we gave him his medicine, but that is all. We both loved Claude.

Rhonda said the arrest "came like a bolt out of the blue. It was the worst thing that ever happened." For someone who had buried as many family members as Rhonda, that was saying something.

Rhonda was born in Lucedale, Mississippi, in 1907, the daughter of a sawmill operator. Her family moved to Mobile when she was very young. She told the *Birmingham News* in 1957 that her parents separated when she was eleven. "I can't think of much happiness I had as a child." Rhonda quit school at fifteen, and soon after, she met W.R. Alderman, a guest at her mother's boardinghouse. They married and then divorced when she was nineteen. At twenty-one, she started dating a neighbor, railroad worker George Garrett. After Garrett died, Talmadge Gibson, who had worked in the "psycho ward" of a VA hospital for six years, wooed the young waitress at a Montgomery café.

I saw all kinds of crazy people, alcoholics and dopeheads and people who had lost their wives. But I ain't never seen a shrewder, more smart person in the whole country than Rhonda Bell.…She ain't no good-looking woman, but she's got personality, and she's smart. I know a crazy person when I see one, and she ain't crazy. The way I figure it is she just likes to see people suffer.

After several dates, Gibson met Rhonda at the Normandy Café, they drank heavily for three days and she brought up marriage. They took a cab to Prattville and got a judge out of bed. They married and were divorced after five months. "I would like to go down there to Montgomery and ask her why she didn't poison me," Gibson told Azbell in 1956. "The only thing I can figure kept her from poisoning me was I was shed of her too quick, or I didn't have no insurance.…Maybe it just wasn't my time." He continued, "I asked her how come all her kids died. I thought there was something funny about all that. Well, sir, she didn't say a word. Sometimes, she would just sit there and look at the kids' pictures and say she wished they were still alive."

As soon as her divorce from Gibson was final, she married Claude, who she had met at the glass factory where she worked. When Claude came down with what Rhonda described as a "nervous disorder" eighteen months into their marriage, Ronald came to help care for his father. That was in February 1951, and Claude was dead in April 1951. She then married

Ronald in December 1951, about ten months after his father died. The marriage to Ronald was illegal under Alabama incest laws, but Rhonda said she didn't know that when they were wed in Prattvillle.

"I'm a poor woman. I've had more than my share of tragedy. Somebody I loved dying almost every year," she told reporters. "I always wanted a home, but looks like every time I get married, there's some tragedy." She said she never wore a dress or shoes that cost more than ten dollars. "I've had tragedy always. I've spent a fortune on medicine."

Her family's medical woes began in 1934, when her daughter Mary Adelaide Garrett, four, died in Montgomery. Rhonda said the child had pneumonia and never walked or talked. In 1937, another daughter, Emogene Garrett, three, died. The child's death certificate, at first, said her death was accidental; Rhonda said it was a heart attack. She later confessed that Emogene's death was a spur of the moment decision when the child was thirsty from playing in the yard and couldn't reach the faucet. Rhonda gave her poisoned milk instead.

In 1939, George Garrett, Rhonda's second husband and the father of her children, died from arsenic-laden whiskey. George came home from work sick and staggered around the backyard. Rhonda soothed him and gave him some whiskey. The next day, he was dead. She later said she placed two teaspoons of arsenic in his coffee for each meal for three months, allowing him to drink it as his three daughters ate beside him. That same year, their daughter Judith, one, also died. Rhonda said Judith died of jaundice. A year later, in 1940, their daughter Carolyn Garrett, six, died from poisoned milk; Rhonda said she had died of a throat disorder. In 1943, Ellyn Elizabeth Garrett, eleven, also died a year after she was left crippled by poisoned milk. After watching the child suffer for months, Rhonda delivered a fatal dose. Rhonda, at first, said Ellyn had died of a stomach disorder. In 1944, Rhonda's mother, Mary Frances Gibbon, died from poisoned coffee, which Rhonda attributed to "infirmities."

Despite that string of mysterious deaths, Rhonda said she had only been arrested twice before, both in the past year, 1955, for drunkenness and reckless driving. Rhonda said she wanted to get back into the church and start a family. "You know what I regret? It's that Ronald and I couldn't have children. We both wanted children, and we couldn't have any. I regret that so much."

Police began investigating Rhonda after Ronald was admitted to a Mississippi hospital a month after being hospitalized in Mobile. A strand of Ronald's hair was tested by federal authorities and found to contain

The victims of Martin—slain daughters Carolyn Garrett, six; Ellyn Elizabeth Garrett, eleven; and Emogene Garrett, three; and husband, Ronald, all paralyzed by poison (shown clockwise from the top left). Courtesy of the Associated Press.

arsenic. The case was worked by rookie Montgomery patrolman T.J. Ward and state investigators Willie Painter, who had investigated the Phenix City corruption that left a candidate for attorney general dead in the street, and Oscar Coley, who followed Rhonda for three weeks in Mobile, eating and chatting with her at her restaurant. The bodies of George and Ellyn Garrett were exhumed, and investigators canvased stores around the state to see if Rhonda had purchased poison.

Painter said that Rhonda had given Claude arsenic three or four times in the months before he died. Rhonda said she received between $3,000 and $4,000 in life insurance on Claude but denied killing Mary and Judith.

Rhonda said she got between $200 and $300 in insurance from each child; $750 and a car from her mother's death; and had set up a $3,000 policy on Ronald. Investigators, however, told the *Montgomery Advertiser* that they thought money wasn't the motive; rather, they thought she believed no one wanted her around. "The more facts we unearthed, the more we realized we were on to something wrong and unusual all the way down the line," Painter told the *Alabama Journal*.

Claude's daughters—Lorraine, a saleswoman at a downtown department store, and Mona Lee, a seventeen-year-old high school student—told the *Alabama Journal* that their brother Ronald, whom they called Bud, was going to be paralyzed from the waist down as a result of her poisoning. They only referred to Rhonda as "the woman." "He never would have married her if she hadn't kept him drunk or doped up," one sister said. "Ronald would come home on leave from the navy, and she would get him drunk....He'd sober up and try to get back to his unit, and she would go out and get more whiskey to keep him drunk. Ronald never went AWOL on his own accord in his life," they said. The two said they loved their "daddy," who was a foreman at Hazel-Atlas Glass Company. "He worked as hard as any of his men, and he worked right alongside them," Lorraine recalled. Rhonda "cried as much as anyone" when he was sick, they said.

While Rhonda had been loving to the sisters while Claude was alive, once he was dead, she was cruel to them, and they both moved out. "Moving when we did probably saved our lives," Mona Lee said. "I have no doubt she meant to poison us, too." When she learned that Rhonda faced the electric chair, Mona Lee said, "They ought to poison her instead."

After being interviewed for twenty-five hours over a period of three days, Rhonda leaned forward and said to police, "I'll tell you....I poisoned them." Rhonda said she never used the same doctor with any of her victims. "I feel like a cloud of fear has been lifted now that I'm caught," she said after confessing, according to the *Montgomery Advertiser*. She told the *Birmingham News* she didn't know why she did it. "I'd do anything to find out why I did it....I loved my children and enjoyed taking care of them....There wasn't enough money involved to do such a thing."

As she awaited trial, Rhonda was reportedly a model prisoner, sewing a beautiful tablecloth for a woman who worked at the Montgomery County Courthouse. A defense witness said Rhonda was schizophrenic, although state witnesses said she was sane. Judge Eugene Carter's comments on schizophrenia prompted Rhonda's attorney to move for a mistrial. Carter said he couldn't pronounce the word and said jurors "don't know what it

Martin awaits execution in June 1956. *Courtesy of the Birmingham News.*

is. I'm not sure I know." "Don't kill this crazy woman. Send her to prison for as long as you can," said court-appointed defense attorney George W. Cameron. Prosecutor William Thetford said that while Claude was "suffering the tortures of the damned, what was she doing? Every now and then, slipping him another shot of the poison....Do your duty and give her the chair."

On June 4, 1956, Rhonda was convicted, and at 11:37 p.m. that Saturday, she was sentenced to death. She collapsed and sobbed. Soon after the verdict was read, Azbell's column, "City Limits," suggested there might be a proposed city ordinance to require autopsies on anyone who died while not under a doctor's care. This is common practice now.

Rhonda met with Governor Big Jim Folsom's legal adviser, E.C. "Bud" Boswell, at the governor's mansion on October 9, 1957, to join a few ministers in a futile request for commutation. Prison officials found a note in her Bible, dated October 14, 1956.

At my death, whether it be a natural death or otherwise, I want my body to be given to some scientific institution to be used as they see fit, but especially to see if someone can find out why I have committed the crimes I have committed. I can't understand it, for I had no reason whatsoever. Can't someone find it and save someone else the agony I have been through?

On October 10, 1957, Rhonda had her final meal: a hamburger, mashed potatoes, cinnamon rolls and coffee. She was strapped into the electric chair at 12:07 a.m. the next morning, and the switch was flipped. Nothing happened. The electrodes hadn't been plugged into the chair. The problem then solved, Rhonda was given 2,200 volts and died three minutes later. She had no final statement, but in a news interview eight days before her execution, Rhonda was asked if she was ready to die. "Well, you've never seen anybody who was ready to sit down in the electric chair. But if that's what it's got to be, that's what it will be."

MARY PERKINS

The world seemed to be ending for Mary Perkins on the morning of Saturday, October 26, 1957, when Selma police were on their way to question her at her house. Mary's two sons and husband were dead, many strange deaths surrounding her were bringing unwanted attention and the many life insurance policies she had on folks without their knowledge cost her nearly $300 a month. So, she grabbed the gun she'd once used to shoot a preacher with whom she'd had an affair. "I thought I'd just kill myself, since I didn't have anything to live for," Perkins told *Jet Magazine*. After a party that was held the night before her son's burial, Perkins packed her dishes, cleaned the house, bathed and dressed in a blue nightgown. "I couldn't kill myself lying down, so I sat up in a chair, took the pistol, and that's the last thing I remember."

Perkins fired a shot into her chest, missing her heart by about an inch. Dr. E.A. Maddox, who treated her gunshot wound, told the *Selma Times Journal* that Mary "didn't seem to realize the gravity of the crime." Maddox said he urged her to confess to police, with a nurse adding she had "a soul to save and a God to face." "Was nothing else to do," Perkins told *Jet Magazine* of her suicide attempt. "I'm only sorry it didn't work."

Perkins confessed to two arsenic poisonings after being charged with three murders and an assault, the *Times Journal* reported. She admitted to killing Gloria Jean Montgomery, the ten-month-old daughter of a friend, and seventy-year-old Della Davis, a longtime friend who was in bad health at the time of her death. She was also charged with killing her husband, Charlie Perkins Sr., in January 1955. Gloria's mother had taken her to Perkins's house and said she was ill and that she needed soda water. Perkins mixed

Mary Perkins (right) is shown as she was escorted to arraingment proceedings before Judge A. J. Hare Thursday to face charges of first degree murder in the alleged poisoning of her husband and Della Davis, an elderly Negro woman. The 36-year-old Selma Negress was brought here from the State Prison for Women at Wetumpka, where she is serving a life sentence for the arsenic poisoning of 10-months-old Negro child Gloria Jean Montgomery. She was escorted from county jail by Deputy Sheriff Richard Holley (left). In the center of the group, walks Byrd Bunkley, Negro, who also faced arraignment for carnal knowledge of a girl under 12 years of age. The cases are slated to be tried before Circuit Judge L. S. Moore during the week of May 12.

Mary Perkins being escorted into court in 1958. *Courtesy of the* Selma Times-Journal.

arsenic with the water, and the child soon died. Davis died on October 7, 1956. Perkins would give her water when she visited.

The assault charge grew from the May 1955 shooting of a janitor and preacher named Menzo Brown. "We started going together [in 1954] before my husband died," she confessed. Perkins grew tired of Brown's control over her. "Every day, at 11 o'clock," Mary told the magazine, "there he would be to get what he wanted—and you know what that was. He would take me in the woods or in the house." When he slapped her, Rhonda shot him in the stomach; Brown, still pastoring three African Methodist Episcopal churches, refused to say who shot him, claiming only that it was a White man. Investigators, while searching her house, found a written confession shuffled away in stacks of papers; in the confession, she admitted to shooting Brown. She said she wrote that hidden confession to get Brown convicted if he killed her. Mary told investigators, in detail, how she tried to shoot Brown with a .32-caliber pistol. Three times, the gun wouldn't fire. "Gun, why don't you shoot?" she said, and then she tried once more, that time, shooting him in the stomach. "You never know who you're going out with when you start slipping around," he said, according to *Jet Magazine*. "I should have told the truth about getting shot....Don't make it too bad about me. I may want to run for the general convention one of these days."

The bodies of Gloria, Della and Charlie were exhumed, and all tested positive for arsenic. The body of Perkins's son, Charlie Perkins Jr., and that of another man, Ed Johnson, were also examined. Perkins had increased the amount of Johnson's life insurance from $250 to $1,300 the day before he died.

Prosecutor Blanchard McLeod assigned two officers to do nothing but track down the people Perkins had insured, as he thought they might have been "walking around carrying loads of arsenic." Investigators knew Perkins had insured at least 84 people. The actual number of insured, police said, could have numbered more than 150, most of them children. Authorities began testing the people Perkins knew who had been sick in the past few months.

Perkins said her thirty-three-year-old husband had accidentally ingested the poison, according to the *Montgomery Advertiser*. "I had the rat poison in the house, and he got into it by mistake." Others she said she poisoned due to greed. "She said in her confession she gave the rat poison to the Montgomery child and Davis because the premiums on some of the other policies was due, and she had no way of meeting the payments," McLeod said. She received $480 for Gloria and $250 for Davis.

Perkins started her scheme by taking out policies on older people, which usually paid out around $500; then she switched to children, which paid as much as $4,000. Another of her possible victims, Ed Johnson, wasn't insured when he died, but after his death, Perkins took out a policy on him.

McLeod would not say how she was able to do that. Marengo County sheriff Wilmer Shields then told AP that they had found a fourth victim, Betty Jean Williams, Mary's ten-month-old grand-niece, who died in Wilcox County. Law enforcement soon exhumed her body, as James Horn, Alabama's superintendent of insurance, said "three or four Selma agents" were being investigated, as were some insurance companies.

Selma's insurance community was suddenly under intense scrutiny, and the list of victims kept growing. Sam Davis, forty-three, and Beulah Moutrie, forty-two, neighbors of Perkins who had died in 1954, were examined. State Toxicologist Vann Pruitt said Mary Lanier, seventy-one, was being treated for arsenic poisoning after Mary visited three weeks earlier and gave her milk. Lanier died in December 1957. Her body was "loaded" with arsenic, the *Selma Times Journal* reported. The recent death of Fannie Kemp, who Mary had insured for $700, was also investigated. The *Huntsville Mirror*, a newspaper for the Black community, said suspicions were growing about the recent deaths of the Reverends A.M. Mosely and Annanias Davis.

As Mary was indicted for three murders, she faced the electric chair. The grand jury chided insurance laws that allowed people to take out life insurance policies on others because it was "dangerous to public safety."

J.E. Harrison, the state manager of Independent Life and Accident Insurance Company, told the *Times Journal*, "There appears to have been laxity in the part of some agent of the company in a situation in which one person was allowed to carry insurance on many others." Harrison continued, "We are as anxious as anyone to get this thing cleared up," An editorial called on the legislature to pass "a necessary law to correct this evil" and criticized the "reckless manner" in which policies were issued. Prosecutor McLeod lashed out at the company, saying it was "impossible for an agent of Independent Life and Accident Insurance Company to operate as he did without the company's knowledge.…Unless the company headquarters chose to completely overlook everything."

The agent in question, Rufus Joseph Hogue, faced four counts of forgery and was to stand trial with Perkins in February. Hogue, a Chilton County native, had been accused of signing off on four applications and suggesting one name. Jack McGee of Chicago sued the company for $30,000 for the death of his grandmother Della Davis about an hour before the indictment. Hogue was still alive at the time of this writing, and his son Joe relayed questions I had about the case. The elder Hogue said he spent one night in jail after being accused of four counts of forgery. The case, however, never went to court because, at the time, what he did was legal in Alabama. "People

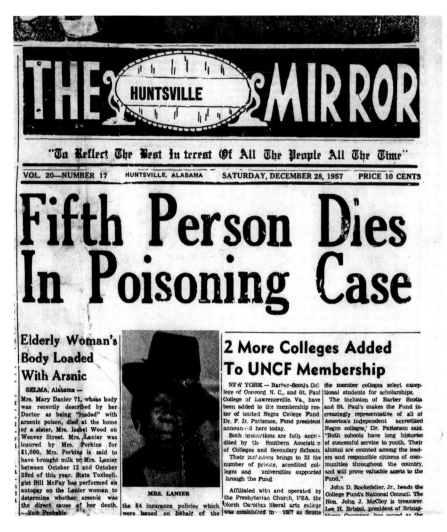

The case of Mary Perkins dominated this front page in 1957. *Courtesy of the* Huntsville Mirror.

could buy life insurance on anyone they want to. He said he changed the law on that," his son told me. "Back then, it was legal, now's it not." Hogue's son said his father may have sold Perkins a few policies but not the hundreds reported by *Jet Magazine*. "He really wasn't involved in the Mary Perkins thing," Joe Hogue said. "*Jet* made it sound like he was in cahoots with her, and he wasn't."

The magazine was a source of news for the Black community, which was largely ignored by White newspapers in Alabama and elsewhere. Although

Perkins's case was, in some ways, more sensational than those of the other three 1950s Alabama poisoners, outside of Selma, the case received little attention, likely because she and her victims were Black. "Had not Mary's son died suspiciously close to the day she increased his insurance, and had not the gentle soul shot herself in a faulty suicide try, more of the living might well have been dead and resting in East Selma Cemetery," *Jet Magazine* reported. The article continued:

> *Lovable Mary Perkins had been nudging her friends and relatives gently toward the grave, mourning at most of their funerals, then drying the tears from her eyes before the bodies were cold. Mary Perkins cooked some of the best food around, was not stingy about feeding the neighbor kids, or carrying plates of goodies to the Ebenezer Church suppers. She nursed the sick with the passion of a Florence nightingale, was a typical minister's wife.*

Perkins told the magazine she was one of twenty-two kids and that her parents had given her "no foundation to build on." On February 26, 1958, the case ended with defense attorney T.G. Gayle calling no witnesses and focusing instead on the "weakness" of the state's case. The jury convicted her after deliberating for two hours that afternoon. She was given ninety-nine years in prison.

What ultimately happened to Mary Perkins is a mystery to me. She said the reason she killed was a mystery to her. "I don't know why I did it. I just got troubled, and something had to happen," *Jet* wrote. "But I didn't kill anybody for the money."

5

TWO WOMEN, SIX MURDERED CHILDREN

The Mattie Smarr and Pearl Griffin Murders

T his is the story of two women, one White, one Black, each battling mental illness, and the six children the two murdered in the early 1950s. One of the women was a mother who feared leaving her children to face a brutal world; the other killed because she dreamed of having a baby of her own. One was sent to a mental hospital for life; the other returned to a quiet suburban Michigan life.

These are the stories of Mattie Smarr and Pearl Griffin.

MATTIE SMARR

Mattie Smarr wanted to share the good news with everyone—she was going to have a baby.

Throughout the spring and summer of 1952, the twenty-seven-year-old woman visited a Jefferson County health clinic, telling the nurses and doctors that she was several months pregnant. On June 24, 1952, the clinic told Mattie there was no baby on the way. That didn't stop her from telling friends and family that she was pregnant. She even bought baby clothes and a bassinet. Mattie, in September, told her mother that she was headed to her mother-in-law's house in the Mount Hebron community of Greene County with her young stepson, Eddie Smarr Jr., to have the baby.

Mattie's brother, Willie Posey, and his wife, Alberta, lived on a farm not far from Smarr's mother-in-law with their children Lucy, twelve; Ola Bee, eight; Ivory, a five-year-old boy; Mattie Jean, two; and three-month-old Cora May. Smarr stayed with the family for a part of the weekend and "rocked the baby a good bit of the time and oiled its skin," Greene County sheriff Frank Lee later said.

Early on the morning of September 22, 1952, the couple went to work in a cotton field and left their children at home. When Willie and Alberta returned home that afternoon, the house was empty. The couple began a frantic search. Lucy was found wandering in a pasture with wounds on her face and head. She couldn't tell them what had happened to her or where little brother and three little sisters were.

Mattie Smarr and three-month-old Cora May. *Courtesy of the Greene County Democrat.*

As the search continued into the night, the bodies of Ola Bee, Ivory and Mattie Jean were found in a creek. The two little girls had drowned, and Ivory had died from a fractured skull. The body of one of the little girls was in the water, while the other was found on some driftwood, resting against a wire fence in the shallow creek. Ivory was found with his face buried in the soft, wet dirt.

Cora May Posey was nowhere to be found.

Once she recovered, Lucy said Mattie Smarr had come to the house around 11:00 a.m., along with Eddie Smarr Jr. Lucy said that Mattie Smarr then took Ola Bee, Mattie Jean, Ivory and Eddie Smarr Jr. fishing. Lucy and Cora May stayed home. Later, Mattie Smarr and all the children returned—except for two-year-old Mattie Jean. Mattie Smarr told Lucy that Mattie Jean was lost; Ivory said the child fell into a creek. Lucy went with Mattie Smarr to search for the child while the others stayed at home. Lucy saw Mattie Jean in the water, and Mattie Smarr told the girl to go help her sister. When Lucy turned, Mattie Smarr pushed her into the creek. The next thing Lucy remembered was waking up in a Demopolis hospital. It's not clear what happened next that Monday afternoon, but Ola Bee soon joined Mattie Jean in the water, and Ivory was dead nearby, with his head bashed in. Mattie Smarr, Eddie Jr. and Cora May were gone.

A posse searched the countryside for two days, hunting the killer. The day after the bodies were found, Mattie Smarr was seen in Eutaw with an infant. Two days after the murders, on the morning of September 24, Mattie Smarr's brother and mother drove her and Eddie Smarr Jr. back to Birmingham. That night, Sheriff Lee, Willie Posey and several officers showed up at Mattie Smarr's Birmingham home. She was in bed with a baby. In the room with them was a newly bought bassinet. She said the baby, with hair that had clearly been recently cut, was her son and had been born the night before. When pressed, Mattie said the baby was given to her by a man. It wasn't long before she laid out the whole ugly truth—she had killed three of her brother's children and abducted his baby daughter. "She apparently had a psychotic desire for a child of her own," Lee said, according to the AP.

Smarr confessed to taking the four children to a creek near their family farmhouse. Mattie Jean was thrown into the water and drowned; Ola was struck in the face with a stick and tossed into the water; Ivory was stuffed into a mudbank, and Mattie Smarr stood on him as he died. Smarr then bashed Lucy's head against sycamore roots.

Willie took Cora Lee back to Greene County that night.

Mattie Smarr's five-day trial was a circus. Pleading not guilty by reason of insanity, Smarr suffered "fits" and displayed "strange behavior" until officers finally tied her to her chair. She refused to talk for three days, kept trying to remove her clothes, appeared to be in a daze and had fainting spells. "Whether Mattie Smarr is executed or confined to an asylum is but incidental," a *Talladega Daily Home* editorial stated. "Whether Mattie Smarr is given absolute justice is one of the most important questions in the world." A jury took just fifteen minutes to convict, and the judge immediately sentenced her to death, sending her to join Earle Dennison as one of only two women awaiting execution in Alabama.

The state supreme court upheld the conviction, even though Smarr's defense attorney was not able to enter testimony from those who said she was known for being "frenzy-minded." Her mother, husband and sisters, however, testified that Smarr started having "fits" or "spells" when she was around ten and that the episodes intensified as she became a teen. Dr. Joe B. Smith, the only doctor called to testify, was a witness for the prosecution, but under cross-examination by the defense, Smith said Smarr was "insane." The judge sustained an objection to the question by the prosecution. Although Smarr had pleaded not guilty by reason of insanity, her attorney called no expert witnesses who could back that claim.

VICTIMS OF GREAT TRAGEDY

EUTAW—Mr and Mrs. Willie Posey of the Mt. Hebron Community of Greene County who suffered the terrible loss of having three of their five children killed, one kidnapped and one critically injured. Mrs. Mattie Smarr, a cousin by marriage of the couple has been indicted for the crime and is now being tried, by a Greene County Circuit Court in Eutaw.

TUSCALOOSA COMMUNITY CHEST TELLS HOW DOLLARS ARE SPENT HERE

The parents of the victims of Mattie Smarr. *Courtesy of the Alabama Citizen.*

Smarr was only spared from death after an examination at Bryce, when Governor Gordon Persons commuted Smarr's sentence to life at Searcy Hospital in Mount Vernon. "She was mentally ill and mentally incompetent at the time of the commission of the crime," three Bryce physicians determined. "She is presently ill and mentally incompetent." The doctors said an "electroence phalographic study" of her brain waves found no brain deformities, the *Alabama Journal* reported.

This wasn't the end of Mattie Smarr's story. In September 1954, Mattie and Lois Wright, a woman convicted in 1950 of killing her mother in Walker County, managed to get ahold of a stolen key, climbed a fence—leaving clothes and personal items behind—and somehow got a ride from the hospital. Wright was captured after a few days, while Smarr remained on the run for nearly two weeks before hospital officers found her at a home outside of Malcolm, about ten miles north of Mount Vernon, on October 4, 1954. I was unable to find out what ultimately happened to Mattie Smarr.

Unlike Smarr, however, Pearl Griffin, another murderer of three children, never went on trial, never faced execution and her life and death weren't wrapped in mystery.

Pearl Griffin

"A distraught mother answered her children's invitation to join them in play yesterday by cutting their throats and slashing herself wildly," AP reported on August 6, 1953. Pearl Griffin, twenty-six, told Marshall County coroner Aubrey Carr her nerves "let go" four months earlier. "Come up and play with us," she supposedly said one child told her.

The dead were Rickey, six; Ronnie, four; and Rosalind, three. Rickey was the first to die, and the other two tried to escape after seeing what happened to him. "Tiny footprints on a blood-soaked floor told the story of their frantic last moments." The gruesome scene unfolded on the upper floor of a converted schoolhouse in Orleander, about seven miles north of Arab, while Pearl's parents were away for a doctor's appointment in Huntsville. Her father, Walter Chaney, said Pearl suffered from a nervous condition. Pearl told the coroner she had repeatedly asked her family to send her to a mental institution and told her husband that she would kill herself. She worried about leaving the kids behind to be "pushed around." Her parents said they had no idea she would hurt the kids.

Pearl's brother, Hosea Griffin, then sixteen, came home and found blood dripping from the ceiling and was said to have heard the feint cry of "papa." Hosea ran upstairs, found the bodies and saw Pearl clutching their father's razor, which she had stolen from his cabinet. Pearl had deep slashes to her left wrist and cuts on her arms, legs, neck and chest. "I killed my children so they would go to heaven. I couldn't leave them behind," she reportedly said.

Horrified, Hosea ran five hundred yards to a store where Imogene Satterfield Barnard worked. A young man, Sammy Wilson, helped Imogene load Pearl into the back of Mildred Perry's pickup truck, and Imogene held the bleeding woman's head in her lap the seven miles to the hospital. "Tell mother and father they know why I did it. I couldn't leave them behind," Barnard said Pearl told her. Coroner Carr later asked Pearl if she knew she "was doing something terribly wrong." Griffin replied, "No, I was going to go through with it." Her husband, Arnold Griffin, twenty-eight, who worked at the Plymouth division of Chrysler, rushed from Michigan to Alabama.

Walter Chaney said Pearl came home to Alabama three weeks earlier on the advice of her doctor and said she was deeply troubled by "religious matters." Dr. J.M. Crawford said Pearl was given blood transfusions just before midnight and had been receiving mental health treatments since returning from Michigan, where she once attempted to kill herself but was

Worried Mother Slays Her Three Children With Razor

Own Wrist Cut, Woman Bares Saga Of Horror

She Did Not Want To Leave Them Behind, Coroner Told

BY AL FUNDERBURKE

A neat attractive 26 year old Marshall county mother who slashed her three childrens throats with a straight razor, then slashed herself and lay beside them to die, was under guard in an Arab hospital today charged with three counts of murder.

Mrs. Pearl Griffin, of Oleander, last night calmly told Coroner Aubrey Carr that she killed her three children "because I didn't want to leave them behind to be pushed around."

Carr said Mrs. Griffin told him the complete story from her hospital bed last night. Speaking just above a whisper, but without any apparent emotion, Carr said, the young mother told of how she took a straight edge razor and cut the throat of six year old Rickey Griffin while the other two children watched horrified. Then as the terrified children tried to escape she caught each of the other two and cut their throat also. All three children were dead when discovered.

Carr said Mrs. Griffin told him she then slashed her own wrist and lay beside the children to die.

Discovered By Brother

The macabre scene was discovered by her brother, 16-year old Hosea Chaney. Entering the living room of the frame house a few miles North of Arab, the boy

MURDER SCENE — The arrow above points to the upstairs attic room where three children were killed by their mother North of Arab yesterday. Dead were Rickey, 6, Ronnie, 4, and Rosaland, 3, children of Mrs. Pearl Griffin. Mrs. Griffin was under guard today in an Arab hospital. Lower left, funeral home attendants load the three bodies into an ambulance. Lower right, the murder weapon. Mrs. Griffin slashed her children's throat with the straight edge razor. The razor was found by Highway Patrolmen Fred Nothdurft and Warren Jones a few feet from the bodies. (Daily Photo)

A large crowd gathers at the family home where Pearl Griffin murdered three children. *Courtesy of the* Birmingham News.

said not to have threatened the children. Pearl was supposed to go with her parents to her mother's doctor but changed her mind at the last minute. "We never thought she'd do anything like this," her father told the *Huntsville Times*.

Arnold Griffin visited his wife before the funerals of his children, which Pearl did not attend. "She's been sick a long time," he told the *Huntsville Times*. The three were buried in white caskets, all in a single grave. Rosalind was in a pink organdy gown in the middle, her brothers on each side. They wore dark blue trousers and white shirts. "Gone to be an angel," read each headstone, with a little lamb on top of each.

The rope held death—Hosea Chaney, 16-year-old brother of Mrs. Pearl Griffin, holds a rope believed used in subduing the children. He is shown where the bodies of the fatally slashed youngsters were found. Blood can be seen on the bedsheets. Mrs. Griffin is accused of killing the children. (Photo by Robert O. Johnson, Albertville.)

At Arab, Ala.—

Mother kills children with straight razor

BY GEORGE WHITTINGTON, News staff writer

ARAB, Ala., Aug. 6—A pretty, 26-year-old mother was

Hosea Chaney, then sixteen, holds a rope that a reporter incorrectly stated was used by his sister, Pearl Griffin, in the murders. To this day, Chaney regrets posing for the picture. *Courtesy of the* Birmingham News.

Pearl told Carr she planned to kill herself because she couldn't afford the medical treatments she was recommended to receive. "I didn't think about the children until a few years ago, but I knew I was going to kill myself and leave them behind. So, I decided to take them with me." She went to church the Sunday before the murders and nearly told a preacher what she was planning. "I decided not to. My family hadn't understood me, and I decided he wouldn't listen either." Dr. J.S. Tarwater of Bryce Mental Hospital said Pearl was insane, the *Huntsville Times* reported. It was also said that people in Michigan got onto her for letting her kids play outside too much.

Hosea Chaney told me the press got many things wrong, like the caption on the photograph of him holding a rope. There was no evidence the kids were tied up, as the *Birmingham News* photograph suggested, and he regretted being in the picture. "We put it behind us. We never really talked about it. It was so devastating," he told me.

After six months of electroshock therapy at Bryce, Pearl went with Arnold back to Michigan. She died on January 31, 2012, at the age of eighty-four in Madison Heights, Michigan, years after her husband died. She worked as a secretary, Hosea said, and he wasn't sure she remembered the murders. "She was bipolar and born that way. I don't think she remembered it well enough to ever bring it up. She functioned real well." Hosea said he thinks God prepared him for what he found that day in 1953. "God talks to us, and I think he prepared me for it. I was sort of ready for it. We knew she had problems. And those children. The kids were just darling. You couldn't have asked for better children."

6
THE TORSO MURDERER
VIOLA HYATT

O n a moonlit summer night, Viola Hyatt drove along Rabbittown Road on a 170-mile journey through four east Alabama counties, across the "whiskey trail," a favorite route of bootleggers. Every so often, Viola tossed from the car one of the severed limbs of the two men she had just brutally murdered. As the sun rose on June 28, 1959, Viola drove the blood-soaked Chevrolet back to her family's White Plains farm, about 15 miles northeast of Anniston. She made a feeble attempt to destroy the evidence of the slayings. Viola Hyatt then went with her father to a church singing, just like they did almost every Sunday, in the same car she had just used to dispose of two bodies.

A young Talladega gospel singer and piano player, Larry Barton, saw the two that day at White Park Heights Baptist Church. I was told by Barton, who served multiple terms as mayor of Talladega, "I told her I thought she looked better than I had ever seen her. She said she had to come see her favorite pianist. As a young girl, she was ugly, obese. People picked on her. She was bullied."

That afternoon, O.P. Holliday decided to pick blackberries near an abandoned Etowah County farmhouse, just as he had the day before. The farmhouse had once been a hotspot for bootleggers and gamblers until a police raid years earlier. Holliday was shocked to find something that wasn't in the farmhouse's desolate driveway the day before—an armless, legless torso covered in a tattered, bloody undershirt.

This composite drawing shows what the "torso murders" victims, then known as Mr. X and Mr. Y, might have looked like in life. *Courtesy of the* Birmingham News.

The next morning, about ten miles away, Mrs. Jack Partlow (I was unable to find her first name) went to check on an unoccupied house she owned about two hundred yards from her own home in St. Clair County's Whitney Junction community. In the driveway, she found a bloody, limbless, shirtless torso. About fifty civil defense volunteers were soon searching for human limbs in two counties, as rumors of "gangland slayings" and a "homicidal maniac" spread like wildfire.

"It's the most gruesome job of killing I ever saw. There is very little blood around the body, so he was not murdered here," Etowah County coroner Noble Yocum told a reporter. "The slayer no doubt cut off the limbs and attempted to destroy the victim's features to prevent identification of the body." Etowah County prosecutor L. Charles Wright told the *Anniston Star*, "I've never seen anything like it around here. Aside from the shotgun blast, his head was pretty well chopped up. Probably with an axe."

The victims, called Mr. X and Mr. Y, were buried on a sloping hill in the Alabama City Cemetery on July 1, 1959. "These men are known only to God and the people who took their lives," said Dr. Denson Franklin of First

Methodist Church. About one hundred people attended the service for men whose names no one knew, unless Viola was in the crowd.

Aside from knowing that they had been killed with shotgun blasts to the head and dismembered, State Toxicologist Robert Johnson said the two probably ate an hour before dying. Mr. Y's stomach contained dried beans, tomatoes, onions and coffee with cream. Mr. X had consumed beef, onions and French dressing. Johnson also found the letters "Ha-per" on the shirt of one of the victims.

Investigators noted that no effort was made to hide the torsos. Gadsden artist John Argyle King and *Birmingham News* editorial cartoonist Charles Brooks drew varying composites of the victims. As the search intensified, the *Birmingham News* asked readers to contact the paper directly with tips, assuring the public they were working closely with police. Divers searched Queenstown Lake, near Trussville, to no avail after an anonymous tip. Detectives scoured the state for the store where one of the victim's undershirt was sold.

The bodies were quietly exhumed and put into a deep freeze for further examination. At the time the bodies were discovered, deep freezing was not a resource typically available to Alabama law enforcement.

"SOMEONE MURDERED AND DISMEMBERED THEM"

The search for the killer and the identity of the victims dragged on for weeks until highway patrol officer Harry Sims, thirty-eight, a twelve-year veteran of the department, began his evening shift on July 15, 1959. Sims swung by the Army Ordinance Depot near Bynum and showed the employees drawings of Mr. X and Mr. Y. Sims was told Mr. Y resembled fifty-five-year-old welder Lee Harper, who had not shown up for work at the depot since July 1. That night, Sims met Patrolman Herman Chapman for coffee, and the two decided to drive down Rabbittown Road. They didn't reach White Plains until 10:00 p.m., and by then, the area's only three stores were closed.

Sims and Chapman kept driving around until 1:00 a.m., an hour after their shift ended. They finally saw someone driving by. The patrolmen flagged down the driver, who said he knew Lee and his brother, forty-eight-year-old bulldozer operator Emmett Harper. However, he had not seen the Harpers since they sat up with a corpse about three weeks earlier. The brothers were both veterans of World War II; Emmett survived the Bataan Death March,

Viola Hyatt peers out of a vehicle in this 1959 photograph. *Courtesy of the Birmingham News.*

the brutal 1942 transfer of captive U.S. servicemen by Japanese forces that led to the deaths of thousands of POWs.

The motorist led the officers to the unpainted, one-story farmhouse on the Hyatts' forty acres of land. The patrolmen took a quick look around, returned to Anniston and radioed the brass in Birmingham. Investigators Ben Allen and A.F. Mason woke up at 2:00 a.m. that Thursday. Just after daybreak, the detectives met the patrolmen, and they went to the Hyatt farm.

Viola Hyatt met the officers at the door and followed them to the trailer that was forty yards behind her house. She told the patrolmen that Lee and Emmett were away on vacation. Investigators noticed that it appeared no clothes had been packed. "Looks as though the Harpers didn't take their clothes with them," Allen said to Viola, according to a news report. "Are you sure they went on vacation?" Viola said the two had gone to Dozier in Crenshaw County, where she said they had family, and that they were building a home there. Viola told police she drove the brothers to catch the late bus at 10:00 p.m. on June 27 and then drove home at 11:00 p.m. and went to bed. That was the night before the first torso was found. Allen noticed the inside of the trailer door was patched with wood cement. "Those Harper boys drink an awful lot. I reckon one of them got high and fired his shotgun at the door," Viola explained, according to a news report. Investigators noticed an old sedan with reddish stains on the seat that someone had apparently tried to clean. Viola said the car was Lee's. A blood-stained hat was found in the front seat.

Left: Investigators examine evidence in the case of Viola Hyatt in Calhoun County in 1959. *Courtesy of the* Birmingham News.

Below: State investigator Arthur Mason flew over St. Clair Etowah and Calhoun Counties looking for clues. *Courtesy of the* Birmingham News.

Sims and Chapman watched as Viola's family ate breakfast, while Allen and Mason went to the nearby home of Alton Hall, who said he and his thirteen-year-old son were awakened by seven to eight shotgun blasts and screams on the night of June 27. Alton said he decided to go back to bed because the Harpers were often drunk and fighting. Gunfire wasn't uncommon, he said, as Viola spent her days shooting rabbits, rats and birds—as well as carrying a knife wrapped in tissue. Alton's wife, however, couldn't go back to sleep and heard a car leave the farm at midnight.

Updated on the investigation, Alabama public safety director Floyd Mann flew that day from Montgomery to Andalusia to show pictures of the victims to Bob Harper, who said he believed they were two of his five brothers—Emmett and Lee. Mann and investigators then flew to Anniston.

Allen confronted Viola at the farmhouse. "Those two men didn't leave this farm alive....Someone murdered and dismembered them here, then took their dismembered bodies out in Lee Harper's car and disposed of them. Miss Hyatt, who was that person?" an article stated. Viola said she knew the answer but was scared to say. Then all three went to Anniston courthouse. Viola cried and pleaded for the detectives not to take her father and stepmother.

"They Never Should Have Hit Her Daddy"

Viola was questioned for hours and at first blamed a former boyfriend, Dewey Carroll, thirty-five, of White Plains. Carroll was brought in for questioning and driven home around 5:00 a.m. on Friday, July 17. "I don't know any more about it than you do," he told the *Alabama Journal*. Around 11:00 p.m. on Thursday, July 16, 1959, the first news report on a break in the investigation went out on WHMA's radio waves. It had been about twenty-four hours since Sims and Chapman started searching White Plains for clues.

Around 2:15 a.m. on Friday, July 17, Viola broke down and told detectives she "had something to show" them. Viola said she had gone to the brothers' trailer that Saturday night. She said Lee was her boyfriend and called her "Sweet," but committed an "unnatural sex act" with her while Emmett threatened her with a knife. Viola said she grabbed a shotgun and shot them in the face as they pleaded for their lives. Lee was shot first, beside the door of the trailer; Emmett was shot as he bent over his dying brother.

She then dragged them outside, dismembered them and discarded them like highway litter. Viola swore to investigators that her parents were asleep and didn't know of the murders. Viola also told detectives that she was driven to murder the two because they mistreated her father, drank too much and argued with her over Lee's car. It was perhaps a violent confrontation that led to the murders. "They never should have hit her daddy," Barton told me.

Barton said that Viola and her father had a strange relationship. "She slept in the bed with her dad until she was thirty." After serving as mayor of Talladega, Barton was convicted of fraud, served three years in prison and was reelected mayor. At the age of seventy-three, his former business partner beat him with a baseball bat at his barbershop in a dispute over an extramarital affair. As of this writing, Barton was working on a book about the murders.

Despite her confession, police were puzzled as to how Viola shot the two, dragged them out of the trailer, dismembered them and scattered their body parts by herself. Viola said she discarded two arms on Sadler Mountain, near Piedmont, and tried to establish alibis, calling the Army Ordnance Depot from a neighbor's phone multiple times asking Lee's boss to have him call her when he got back from his vacation. The plant also received a call from a woman asking to extend his vacation.

"I feel better," she reportedly said after confessing. As she was questioned, Lee's Chevrolet was parked outside the jail, and people gathered to look at the bloodstains in the backseat. While her father, M.B. Hyatt, was questioned, Viola's stepmother slept in a police car. Detectives set up an improvised lab at the farm to test the blood that was found outside of the trailer and on the floor inside.

Viola took investigators on a three-hour trip through Etowah, Calhoun and St. Clair Counties, retrieving two arms and two legs she had thrown from the car, and then she led police back to her father's farm. Two legs were found in brush on U.S. 11 in Etowah County, and two arms were found several miles away. A fisherman on the Tallapoosa River spotted a third leg near Bell's Mill Bridge, eight miles east of Heflin. Viola said she threw two legs off that bridge. Viola showed police the spot in a cornfield where she had buried the axe she had used to cut up the bodies and the wheelbarrow she had used to ferry the body parts to Lee's car. "Where's my axes?" M.B. Hyatt asked police, the *Montgomery Advertiser* reported. They had been taken by a toxicologist. The highway patrolman assured him that he would get them back. "There never has been no blood on that axe," he fired back. It was about the only emotion he showed. "I don't believe she did it. She might have done it—I don't know."

Hyatt's father and stepmother on their porch. *Courtesy of the* Birmingham News.

As news of the confession spread, hundreds gathered at the Hyatts' farm. Neighbors described Viola as a "friendly, jolly person. A little different but as nice as she could be," the *Alabama Journal* reported. For three weeks after the murders, Viola drove Lee's car along Rabbittown Road, waving to neighbors. Police searched the Hyatts' property in the rain, reporters Howell Talley and Clyde Bolton wrote for the *Gadsden Times*.

"I don't see how I can get through the world without my girl. That's what hurts me," M.B. Hyatt told them. "I couldn't stand him," M.B. said of Lee Harper to the *Montgomery Advertiser*. "He would get mad at you before you could say scat. He was all the time wanting to kill somebody." Hyatt said he had to break up late-night fights and that Emmett had once come running to the house, blood streaming down his face. Lee had stomped his brother's face and dragged him down a highway. Hyatt said he didn't charge the Harpers rent because they let them take the car to Sunday singings. Lee used to go with them but stopped after he got blackout drunk in Jacksonville and some boys who found him sleeping in the woods mistook him for dead.

"I told him I would kill him if he laid a hand on her, and I meant it, too," Hyatt said of Lee's threat to beat up Viola. Hyatt was forty-five years old when Viola, thirty at the time of her arrest, was born. Viola's biological mother was a "hellion" who hated living on a farm, Barton said. "She told [Viola] she should have fed her to the hogs when she was born." Stroking Viola's yellow tabby cat, Hyatt said he and his wife heard no gunshots that night and thought nothing of the three-week disappearance. "What's wrong, Daddy?" Viola said, interrupting the interview. She had been brought back to the farm by lawmen. "Daddy, I don't want you talking to newspapermen." He replied, "I ain't said nothing but the truth." But she led him away by the arm, and the interview was over.

Before they took Viola back to jail, she put on an orange dress and her best white shoes and said goodbye to her family, dog and seven cats. She took one last pensive look at the family farmhouse, and the police drove her away. When Viola was taken back to the jail around 9:15 p.m., she carried a bundle containing a spare dress, although there were murmurings in the crowd it was an arm or a leg.

"THE CHAIR OR LIFE"

As the trial neared, Viola read newspapers and had one visit from her father. Her defense team said the best they could hope for was saving Viola from execution. "The only issues we could see were whether she got the chair or life," said her court-appointed attorney, R.A. Norred. On March 14, 1960, just before 11:35 a.m., Viola changed her plea from not guilty by reason of insanity to guilty. She was sentenced to life in prison.

Her defense attorneys said Viola would not give them a motive. "I had the best reasons in the world," she supposedly said. It wasn't sexual abuse but "something much worse" that drove her to murder, she said. Viola and her father embraced at the end of the trial. "I'll tell ya this: I'm a-gonna get her out of there if I live," Hyatt told the *Birmingham News*.

Calhoun County sheriff Roy Snead returned evidence to the victims' brother, Joe Harper—a guitar with a pawn shop tag, an alarm clock, a trailer hitch, two razors and ten dollars in cash.

A year after the murders, in 1960, Viola was settled in at Tutwiler Prison. "She gets along fine with the other women, and she has joined our softball team. She is the scorekeeper," said prison superintendent Edwina Mitchell. Viola also worked a sewing machine in the garment factory. That year, she was permitted to visit her sick father, escorted by a prison guard, at Anniston's Memorial Hospital, and in 1961, she was allowed to attend his funeral.

Viola was paroled in 1970, after spending a decade as an "exceptionally good" inmate. She lived a quiet life until she died at the age of seventy-one in June 2000. She never gave an explanation for the crime and never granted interviews on the grisly "Torso Murders." She never said if anyone helped her. "She went to her grave keeping that to herself," Barton told me.

7

PATRICIA KRENWINKEL

Mobile's Manson Family Murderer

Patricia Krenwinkel turned twenty-two in a Mobile jail cell, the first of at least fifty birthdays she celebrated behind bars. That birthday, Mobile police sergeant Sam McLarty sent her fingerprints to the Los Angeles Police Department (LAPD) and linked her to some of the most shocking crimes in American history.

McLarty and Mobile police detective Sergeant John W. "Bill" McKellar, two days earlier, on December 1, 1969, went to the southwest Mobile home of Patricia's aunt Garnett Reeves. For their counterparts in California, time was running out. LAPD chief Edward Davis was planning a press conference that afternoon to announce that warrants had been obtained in the Tate-LaBianca murders, an announcement that would launch Charles Manson and his "family" into eternal notoriety. Los Angeles prosecutor Vincent Bugliosi feared that if Patricia learned she was charged in the murders, they might never apprehend her. The two Mobile officers didn't find Patricia at her aunt's house but saw a sports car drive past. A teenage boy was behind the wheel, and a young female passenger suddenly pulled down her floppy, black felt hat to cover her face. McLarty and McKellar made a U-turn and stopped the car. Patricia told the police her name was Marnie Montgomery but finally admitted it was Krenwinkel when she was taken to her aunt's house. The boy was questioned and released.

Patricia was taken into custody and read her rights at 3:20 p.m., about forty minutes before Davis was scheduled to announce the charges. Reeves

Krenwinkel with her Mobile lawyer, the late M.A. "Bubba" Marsal, pictured in 1969 after she was arrested on a murder warrant and just before her twenty-second birthday. *Courtesy of Mobile's* Press-Register.

said Patricia was "a very sweet girl and a Christian girl" and "was very interested in the Bible. She often talked about it and studied it," *UPI* reported on December 3, 1969—Patricia's birthday. "She just liked people too much to do anything like that," Reeves said when asked if Patricia was involved in the seven murders. "She is a very nervous, frightened, and confused young woman," said Patricia's attorney, James Atchison.

The next day, Patricia told the *Press-Register* she knew nothing of the chilling California killings of actress Sharon Tate and six others over two nights. She refused, on the advice of her lawyer, to discuss the charges against her or the previous two years of her life. "I probably enjoy music and nature most of all. I like to wander around and just see what God gave us," Patricia told the reporters. She told them she loved the Beatles and the Bible. "I like living in Mobile. It's beautiful."

Patricia's life had changed two years earlier, in September 1967, when the nineteen-year-old met Manson at a party and three days later walked away from her job as a file clerk, abandoning her car and paycheck. She got into a Volkswagen bus with thirty-three-year-old Manson and her new family and disappeared. Patricia used her credit card to fund the family's journey and went by the aliases Katie, Marnie Reeves, Big Patty and Mary Ann Scott. Along the way, Dennis Wilson of the Beach Boys picked up Patricia while she was hitchhiking, and soon, Charles Manson was in his world, kissing the drummer's feet in front of others and bringing the family to live off of him in 1968.

This front page from December 2, 1969, shows Krenwinkel and Tex Watson saying they were part of a "savage mystic cult." *Courtesy of the* Los Angeles Times.

The night Patricia took off with Manson, her father, California insurance agent Joseph Krenwinkel, asked Patricia's half-sister about the mysterious man. "I am convinced he was some kind of hypnotist. It was all so spontaneous," Joseph told the *Los Angeles Times*. "I soon learned he wasn't the most savory character in the world."

"You Did Wrong"

Patricia was born in Los Angeles in 1947. Her parents divorced when she was seventeen, and she spent much of her time with her mother in Mobile, attending Theodore High School for two months and finishing the eleventh grade there before going back to Los Angeles. She spent a semester at Spring Hill College, a Mobile-based Jesuit school, where she became interested in religion and the Bible. She later wrote to a professor there each day from jail. In 1967, she moved into a Manhattan Beach cottage in California with her half-sister.

"I am going to find myself," Patricia wrote to her father in a letter postmarked from Seattle two weeks after she left her job and "defected from the middle class," as a news article would later say. Weeks later, Joseph's ex-wife Dorothy called and said Patricia had contacted her. Patricia said she was living in Sacramento and wanted one hundred dollars. Joseph tracked down his daughter's phone number and offered her a ticket back to Alabama. "She said no, she wanted the money. I said I wouldn't send any," he reportedly told the *Los Angeles Times*.

After that, Joseph Krenwinkel didn't hear from Patricia for two years until the Los Angeles County sheriff told him that she was being held in the stabbing death of a man who had befriended some hippies. This was just two months after seven people were butchered in a two-night rampage that horrified the nation. Not knowing the full scope of the accusations facing Patricia, her father took her home from jail. "During our drive back to Inglewood, I was concerned. Her response was so unemotional. I don't think we spoke 20 words by the time we hit the San Diego Freeway," he told the *Los Angeles Times*.

They stopped for a bite to eat, and she opened up, though she said nothing about any murders. Joseph said he was convinced all was well. "I'm not the kind to use the third degree. I didn't want to preach, 'You did wrong.' I didn't think I could win her back that way." She reportedly told her father in a phone call to his office a week after that drive home from jail, "I'd like to go home and see mother." He bought her plane ticket to Alabama. In a matter of weeks, Patricia was in a Mobile jail cell, fighting to keep from returning to California and standing trial in one of the most sensational murder cases of the twentieth century.

"EMOTIONALLY DISTURBED, PROBABLY PSYCHOTIC"

Spending the last Christmas season of the 1960s in a Mobile jail cell, Patricia's name was in newspapers and TV broadcasts around the world. Fingerprints that were taken from her in Mobile showed that Patricia's left little finger was a match for a print taken from the inside of a blood-splattered French door that led from murdered actress Sharon Tate's bedroom to a swimming pool.

Patricia's attorney, M.A. "Bubba" Marsal, argued that the extradition orders were not valid because they were signed by the lieutenant governor, not California governor Ronald Reagan. Marsal said that as far as Alabama knew, the extradition filing could have come from "the quarterback for the Los Angeles Rams," and he argued that Patricia should be released. Alabama governor Albert Brewer signed off on the request to send her to California, and Mobile County district attorney Carl Booth was fighting to fly her from lower Alabama to Los Angeles.

Squeaky Fromme, the Manson family member who tried to assassinate President Gerald Ford in 1975, sent Patricia letters throughout her holiday season incarceration in Alabama. "Together, we stand….If you go extra is good," one letter read, according to *Helter Skelter: The True Story of the Manson Murders*, which Bugliosi wrote with Curt Gentry.

Patricia's mother visited her in jail. "I tried to ask her why all this happened, and she would just blow me a kiss and look sort of vague," Dorothy said, according to *UPI*. "I still love her and will always love her. And nobody can ever tell me she did anything horrible."

On Christmas Eve 1969, Patricia was visited in the Mobile jail by psychiatrist Dr. Claude Brown, whose report was cited by defense witness Dr. Andre Tweed. "She was exceedingly afraid of Charles finding her and killing her," the report said. "She says that she will never be able to get away from him, that there is no place to run or hide." Brown wrote that Krenwinkel "showed a schizophrenic reaction…impaired judgment and auditory hallucinations," and he said that at the time of the murder, she was possibly "emotionally disturbed, probably psychotic."

Patricia received a telegram in jail on December 29, 1969. "In L.A. call attorney Reiner 665-129 and wherever, together, love is." The message was signed "Squeaky, Sandy and Everybody." Ira K. Reiner was already representing some of the family. Sandy was most likely Sandra Good, a Manson family member who was sent to prison in the 1970s for death threats that she mailed to corporate executives she believed were destroying the environment.

This August 1970 photograph shows Manson family followers (*from left to right*) Susan Atkins, Patricia Krenwinkel and Leslie Van Houten walking to court. *Courtesy of the Associated Press.*

Patricia fired her attorney, M.A. Marsal, about two months later and told the district attorney she wanted to go back to California. She got her wish on February 20, 1970. "Dressed in a camel-colored plaid wool dress, wearing black leather shoes and carrying a cream-colored wool coat, Miss Krenwinkel walked freely between two police officers from Los Angeles, who came to Mobile Wednesday to take her to the West Coast to stand trial on seven counts of murder," a reporter wrote. "In a brief farewell to her relatives, Miss Krenwinkel kissed and hugged both of them just before being led to the plane. Silently walking to the plane, with only a trace of a smile, she ignored questions by newsmen."

Four months later, on June 20, 1970, Patricia's twenty-nine-year-old half-sister, Charlene Ann Lowell, drank whiskey with Bennie Fred Mosley, twenty-six, and swam in Mobile's Halls Mill Creek. It wasn't far from where Patricia had stayed with her aunt and uncle. Bennie fell asleep, and when he woke up, Charlene was gone. He and Charlene's uncle William Leroy Reeves found her dead in the water that Sunday morning, and they found her swimsuit on a nearby shore. Mobile County coroner Earl Wert said Charlene had mysterious bruises, and he ruled out drowning because there was no water in her lungs. The state toxicologist determined that her death was due to a mixture of alcohol and an "undetermined" drug. Charlene was a heroin addict, according to Bugliosi, and had given Patricia diet pills, barbiturates, mescaline and LSD when she was a teen. To this day, Manson family conspiracy theorists speculate Charlene was murdered.

"THERE WAS BLACKNESS AND THAT WAS ALL"

When Patricia took the witness stand on February 19, 1971, a year after her extradition, Manson raised his left arm and extended his left index finger. Codefendants Susan Atkins, Leslie Van Houten and Krenwinkel soon did the exact same thing. "I've taken so much acid; I am acid," she testified as she pointed at the ceiling. "I never come down."

Patricia claimed that she, Tex Watson, Atkins and Linda Kasabian "dropped acid" on August 8, 1969, and went for a drive with no intention to kill. In her Mobile jail cell, however, Patricia said she was "coming down" from drugs and had not taken any on the night of the murders. She would testify at a future parole hearing that she left with the group with instructions from Manson to do whatever Watson said. Regardless of whatever else happened that night, they ended up at Tate's home on Cielo Drive.

The twenty-six-year-old pregnant wife of filmmaker Roman Polanski, who was away making a movie, was there with her former lover, Birmingham native and celebrity hairstylist Jay Sebring. Also, there was coffee heiress Abigail Folger and Wojciech Frykowski, an aspiring screenwriter and friend of Polanski. Steven Earl Parent, eighteen, who was visiting the estate to sell a clock radio to a caretaker, was the first of the five killed. "I had a knife in my hand, and she ran out the back door," Patricia said of killing Abigail Folger. "I chased her through the door, onto the lawn, and I stabbed her, and I kept stabbing her, and I looked up, and there was blackness, and that was all," she said. Patricia complained to her fellow family members that her hand hurt from her knife striking bones, court records state. When asked if she felt anything after stabbing Folger, Patricia replied, "Nothing. It was just there and like it was right." And as they left, Patricia said she felt "complete paranoia."

The next night, Manson led the four murderers, plus Van Houten and Steve "Clem" Grogan, to the Waverly Drive home of grocery executive Leno LaBianca and Rosemary LaBianca, who co-owned a dress shop. Patricia stabbed Rosemary and carved "war" in Leno's chest. She left a carving fork sticking out of his stomach and a steak knife in his throat. Krenwinkel wrote in blood "Rise" and "death to pigs" on the walls and "Healter [*sic*] Skelter" on the refrigerator door.

While on the stand, Patricia called Manson "perfection" and the best lover she ever knew. Her parents testified for the defense, fighting to keep her out of the gas chamber, while Patricia shouted objections. Joseph Krenwinkel showed off her baby pictures and report cards and described his daughter as an "exceedingly normal child, very obedient." "I love her and will stand by her. I feel the same way I did about her the day she was born," said Dorothy Krenwinkel. "She loved to play on the swings and with her stuffed animals and with other children," Joseph added. They showed off a picture of her with six chicks the Easter Bunny had brought her in 1951. "They all grew up, every one of them," her mother chuckled. "We had to give them away because we couldn't kill them. Pat had given them all names." Patricia once dented the fender of mother's car to avoid hitting a dog. "She would rather harm herself than any living thing," her mother said. "She wanted to go to a Jesuit school because she wanted think about her religious background," Dorothy added. "She taught vacation Bible school from the time she was ten-years-old and always enjoyed church activities so much." Joseph said, "I couldn't have asked for a better daughter."

But that all changed when she met Manson, they said. "She was like a stranger. I couldn't talk to her," Dorothy said. "It was her association with those people," Joseph said.

"THE UNENDING SUFFERING OF THE VICTIMS"

Patricia didn't make it easy to keep her out of prison. She interrupted her attorney and demanded he be removed from the case. "I have talked with him about the way I wish this to be handled right now, and he doesn't do as I ask," she told the judge. "He is to be my voice, which he is not." The judge refused to remove her attorney.

Bugliosi speculated that Manson was quietly pulling the strings of the defense attorneys for the women he wanted to take the fall. Krenwinkel, Atkins and Van Houten, at one point in the trial, lit matches in their cells, heated bobby pins and burned X-marks on their foreheads, Bugliosi wrote. They then ripped open the burnt flesh with needles, leaving a jarring impression for the jurors who were returning to court the following Monday morning.

"Patricia Krenwinkel is twenty-three years old," her attorney, Paul Fitzgerald, argued before the jury went to decide its verdict. "With 365 days in the year, there are approximately 8,400 days in twenty-three years, and approximately 200,000 hours in her lifetime....The perpetration of these offenses took, at best, approximately three hours. Is she to be judged solely on what occurred during three of 200,000 hours?"

Patricia, Charles and other members of the Manson family were eventually convicted. "You have just judged yourselves," Krenwinkel said when Charles was sentenced to death. "Better lock your doors and watch your own kids," Atkins added. "Your whole system is a game. You blind, stupid people. Your children will turn against you," Van Houten told the jury.

In prison, Krenwinkel earned a college degree, played on the prison softball team and trained inmates to fight fires. In 1988, Krenwinkel was said to have told her prison psychiatrist that Folger "could have been something more than she was, a drug abuser." She has disputed Manson's claim that he did not order the murders. When Atkins died in 2009, at the age of sixty-one, Krenwinkel became the longest-serving female inmate in the California prison system. Her father visited her in prison and helped her realize "what had happened, and the monster I became....Everything that was good and decent in me, I threw away," she said in 2011. "I am someone you would never have wanted to be, and here are the steps you can take to never go to the dark places I have been," she said she told young people.

The parole board was not moved in 2011, when she said she took part in the murders because she was turned into a "monster" by Manson. "The panel finds it hard to believe a person can participate in this level of crimes and can't identify anything but 'I wanted him to love me,'" parole commissioner Susan Melanson said as Krenwinkel wept profusely. "This is a crime children grow up hearing about." Krenwinkel was denied parole for the fourteenth time in 2017, the same year Manson died in prison at the age of eighty-three. At that hearing, Patricia argued that she had committed the murders because Manson physically and emotionally abused her, trafficking her to other men for sex. "I thought I loved him. I thought—it started with love and then turned to fear," she said. Tate's sister, Debra Tate, fought the parole effort. "She has no insight into the crime and is still minimizing her offense," Debra Tate said in 2017.

Patricia will again be eligible for parole in 2022. She has said she is very concerned that young people "seem to think that what we did was all right. There is nothing, nothing that we did that is all right."

"I'm just haunted each and every day by the unending suffering of the victims, the enormity and degree of suffering I've caused," she said in the 2011 parole hearing. "I'm so ashamed of my actions. The victims had so much life left to live."

8

MARIE HILLEY

The Black Widow of Anniston

Shivering from four days in the bitter cold, Audrey Marie Hilley flailed at the door of a stranger's home, barely a mile from her Blue Mountain birthplace. When Hilley died that evening in 1987, she left behind a legacy of misery and murder—and mysteries that may never be solved.

Two women, Sue Craft and Janice Hinds, on seeing Hilley's struggle, shuffled through the February rain to help the disheveled woman. They had no idea they were watching the life slip away from one of Anniston's most infamous murderers. "I really didn't like looking at her. She was scary. There were spots of mud on her face. Her bangs were stuck to her forehead. She had long fingernails, like she had never wrung out a mop," Craft later told the *Anniston Star*.

Hilley told them her name was Sellers, that her car had broken down and that she had walked, then crawled, to the porch. Craft didn't recognize Hilley, although she had graduated from Anniston High School in 1950, a year before her now-dying former classmate, and the two had lived a stone's throw apart. Craft and Hinds didn't recognize Hilley from eight years of frontpage stories and news broadcasts. "Her hands were pinkish blue and purplish. She had one shoe on and one shoe off, and she was holding the shoe that was off and once tried to put it back on but couldn't," Hinds told the newspaper. "She looked like such a dignified lady [on TV], and to think that all this happened. I just hope she had time to make it right with the Lord."

Marie Hilley arrives at the Atlanta airport in 1983, after being extradited to face charges in Alabama. *Courtesy of the* Anniston Star.

At Anniston's Regional Medical Center, Hilley died at the age of fifty-three. Her life was a trail of deceit, destruction and false identities, stretching from Texas to Vermont, inspiring a Lifetime movie and true crime shows from America to Japan. She was pronounced dead at the same hospital, where her husband, Frank Hilley, had died twelve years earlier and where her daughter nearly died in 1979. Hilley died of a hypothermia-induced heart attack while making a desperate run from a sentence of life plus twenty years in prison. Her husband and daughter were victims of Marie's arsenic-laced meals and injections she falsely told them would cure them of the suffering she was secretly inflicting on them. They may not have been the only ones to have suffered that fate.

In 1975, Frank was painfully aware of Marie's extramarital affairs, and yet, he was seemingly ignorant of her lavish spending. He began to suffer from a mysterious illness a doctor diagnosed as a stomach virus. In May of that year, Marie and Frank went to visit their son, Michael, in East Point, Georgia. During the visit, Frank "seemed tired and sluggish. He wasn't feeling too well," according to Michael's testimony years later inside a packed Calhoun County courtroom. A few days later, Frank's sister Frieda Adcock went to visit Frank and found him in agony. "I'm sicker than I've ever been in my life. If something's not done for me, I won't be here long," Frank told Adcock.

At 3:30 that morning, Frank was wandering his yard in his underwear, saying he was looking for his car. He was taken to a hospital, where he died three days later, on May 25, 1975, at the age of forty-five. It appeared he had died from what was then labeled infectious hepatitis.

Michael watched a nurse remove an IV from his father's arm, leaving behind purple streaks three to four inches long. It struck Michael as odd; the nurse told him she had never seen anything like it. "It never left my mind." It was not the first time Michael sensed "something wasn't right" with his family, and it would not be the last.

"You Hoped It Wasn't True"

Marie Hilley was born in 1933, and at the age of seventeen, she married Frank while he was on leave from the U.S. Navy. Michael was born a year later and his sister, Carol, was born in 1959. "There were always expressions of love, yet there was always something unsettled in the back of my mind regarding [Marie]," Michael Hilley told me. "I always sensed something wasn't right, but you hoped it wasn't true. That was our normal, so we didn't have anything to compare it to."

Soon after Frank's death, Marie cashed in a $31,140 life insurance policy and went on a spending spree, even buying Carol a motorcycle. Michael once watched his sister get ready to take a ride with his mother, and his eyes met Marie's eyes when she got on the back. "In that brief second, I knew that she had something to do with my father's death, and I could see she knew that I knew," Michael said. "I saw in her, after that, an escalation to cover things up, and I didn't ask her questions because I knew I would get a lie."

Soon, Marie began bombarding the Anniston Police Department with reports of vandalism and threatening phone calls. Police would tap her phone and hear nothing unusual, and as soon as they stopped, Marie would report more calls. The house burned on multiple occasions. All evidence pointed toward Marie as the culprit. "You want to attribute it to her having just lost her husband, but you sensed it was something deeper," Michael said.

Frank's sister Frieda Adcock said years later that Marie soon grew restless, moving with Carol every few months. She also said that Marie would "watch herself in the bathroom mirror all night." While living with one relative, Marie slept on a couch with a crowbar and gun underneath and would leave only to return with large amounts of cash. "Carol has said she would wake up and find her mother standing over her," Adcock said. Michael said Marie would talk about people coming after her for his dad's gambling debts, which Michael thinks were nonexistent. "Most of that was her imagination at work, trying to cover her tracks." It fit a pattern Michael had seen her display his entire life.

Marie had been self-centered and narcissistic since childhood. As an adult, she would fake illnesses at special occasions, he said. "She had to take the focus off someone else and put it back on herself. It was all about making the focus on her." Marie brought attention to herself in 1979 by nearly killing her daughter. This sent Marie on a bizarre, downward spiral that found her running from the law and adopting a fake identity—and creating a twin sister for her fake identity.

A year earlier, Marie took out a $25,000 life insurance policy on Carol. Carol was suffering from severe nausea by April 1979, and for months, she was frequently in the emergency room. Marie gave Carol a shot in her hip in August 1979, and her daughter began experiencing numbness in her fingers and legs. After Carol was admitted to Anniston's hospital, doctors could not determine the cause of her numbness and sent her to Birmingham's Carraway Methodist Hospital for a psychiatric evaluation. While there, Marie gave Carol two injections she said she had bought from a nurse, and she made Carol promise not to tell anyone. Carol was soon at University Hospital, no longer able to walk or dress herself. A doctor noticed white lines in Carol's fingernails and realized she had been poisoned.

On the day Carol was admitted to that hospital, September 18, 1979, Marie was arrested for writing $6,000 in bad checks. A few days later, Calhoun County coroner Ralph Phillips received a letter from Michael. "It is my belief that she probably injected my dad with arsenic, as she has probably done my sister," he wrote. Michael Hilley had reason to suspect that he nearly met the same fate as his father. He would later testify that, in the summer of 1979, he and Marie had argued over a $50,000 stock certificate. "I told her that right after breakfast, we were going to go down to the bank and were going to get it straightened out." Ten minutes after breakfast, Michael began vomiting so strenuously he had to see a doctor.

"I DID NOT GIVE MY DAUGHTER POISON"

Still in jail for the bad check charges, Marie was interviewed for more than two hours on September 26, 1979, by Anniston police lieutenant Gary Carroll, who'd had to contend with her phony threat complaints and legitimate complaints from businesses who wanted money Marie owed them. This time, he was interested in what had made Carol Hilley so ill.

During the interrogation, Marie admitted that she had twice injected Carol with the antinausea medicine Phenergan. She also admitted to giving her own mother, Lucille Frazier, injections fifteen months after Frank died. Lucille was soon dead herself. Marie denied any wrongdoing. "I did not give my daughter poison. It never entered my mind," Hilley told Carroll. "I don't think I could do anything like that. Nobody could make me believe I would—not to my children, not to anyone else....And, if I did do something like that, I don't think I'd care much about living anymore. Nobody can ever make me believe I did anything to hurt Carol."

Frank Hilley's body was exhumed on October 3, 1979. Arsenic tests showed his hair contained ten times the normal level of arsenic, and his toenails contained one hundred times the normal level. The poison had likely been administered over several months. The cause of death was changed to acute arsenic poisoning. Vials that were soon found in Marie's home and purse both contained arsenic.

Marie was arrested for the attempted murder of her daughter. Despite the cloud of suspicion, a group of Anniston residents paid Marie's $14,000 bail. She checked into the Rodeway Inn in Homewood under the name Emily Stevens, and she was to meet her attorney there on November 18, 1979. When he arrived, Marie was gone, but there was a note that suggested Marie had been kidnapped. Police dismissed it as another lie. Marie, now a fugitive from justice, was indicted in Frank's death.

This is where the story gets weird.

John Homan, in February 1980, was enjoying a drink in Fort Lauderdale, where he ran a boat-building business, when he met a captivating Texas widow named Robbi Hannon, who said she was suffering from a life-threatening illness. Coming out of a bad marriage, Homan believed everything Hannon said. By that summer, they had moved to Marlow, New Hampshire, together. The two married; she worked as a secretary, and for two years, they lived a quiet life, staying for a time with a woman named Marie Champagne. "She came on to you as an understanding and loving type," Champagne would later say. "She was a beautiful person."

Carol Hilley arrives at the courthouse in Anniston for her mother's trial. *Courtesy of the Alabama Department of Archives and History, donated by Alabama Media Group.*

Robbi went to Texas in September 1982, and told John she was visiting her twin sister, Teri Martin. In November, Teri called John to tell him Robbi had died. Months later, Teri came to see John in New Hampshire, twenty pounds lighter than Robbi, with a personality unlike her sister's and with bleached hair. Teri soon took Robbi's place in John's life. Teri went to work for a publishing company in Battleboro, Vermont, and she and Homan ran an obituary for Robbi, saying her body was donated to the Medical Research Institute in Texas. Coworkers were suspicious of "Teri," and it was soon discovered that there was no Medical Research Institute in Texas.

"A COLD, CALCULATING, CUNNING KILLER"

Confronted by police and the FBI on January 12, 1983, Teri admitted that she was Marie Hilley. "I never knew she was a dual personality," Robert March, who hired both Robbi and Teri through his employment agency, later told the *Anniston Star.* "She was a very personable, efficient person who tested well."

Robin DeMonia, a former *Birmingham News* colleague of mine who covered the case for the *Anniston Star*, said Homan told her he believed

Marie kept secrets to try and protect him. "There was aloofness, things she wouldn't talk about," Homan told DeMonia. "I feel that the woman was trying to get out of my life to get me out of the mess I eventually went through." He said that Marie once explained, "If I cared for you, I wouldn't want you to go to jail, and if I told you, you'd be aiding and abetting." Homan thought Marie created the twin sister to get money to run away. "Another week and she would have been gone," he told DeMonia. "The night she was arrested, she didn't expect to ever see me again. It would have been a lot easier to walk away. But I cared. It was something that was important and special to me."

DeMonia said she thinks Homan was taken in by Marie's good looks. "The people who liked him thought he wasn't an attractive man. He was a lonely guy," she recalled. Marie was soon on her way back from New England to answer for the death of her husband and the poisoning of her daughter. Crowds lined up outside the courthouse to hear the lurid details. "You're not dealing with your average, ordinary housewife. You are dealing with a cold, calculating, cunning killer.…She's like a black widow spider," prosecutor Joseph D. Hubbard said in his closing argument. The jury convicted and sentenced Marie Hilley to life plus twenty years in prison.

But the story wasn't over.

District Attorney Robert Field suspected that Hilley had poisoned Frank and Marie's mothers and possibly several other people. The bodies

Marie Hilley smiles as she arrives at the courthouse in Anniston for her trial. *Courtesy of the Alabama Department of Archives and History, donated by Alabama Media Group.*

of Frank's and Marie's mothers were exhumed. Marie's mother's body contained ten times the normal level of arsenic. Her death was still ruled to be a result of cancer. Frank's mother, who died the day Marie fled in 1979, had significant levels of arsenic, but they were not fatal. The body of one of Carol's friends, eleven-year-old Sonya Marcelle Gibson, was exhumed in September 1983 and tested for poison. Sonya had died suddenly on February 1, 1974, while aboard a medical helicopter that was flying from a Fort McClellan hospital to Birmingham for treatment. That examination confirmed the original ruling that Sonya had died from a viral heart infection and inflammation.

For three years, Marie sat in prison, her victims pulled their lives back together and Anniston put the dark episode in the past. Homan moved into the Heart of Anniston Inn, a rental flophouse, to make a two-and-a-half-hour drive to visit the woman he had known as Robbi, Teri and Marie. The warden even gave Marie a few eight-hour passes from the prison.

"Give Me an Hour to Get Out of Town"

On Thursday, February 19, 1987, Marie Hilley was given a three-day pass. Marie told Homan she was going to visit her parents' grave. It was the only time she had "blatantly lied" to him, he told DeMonia. Homan waited in vain for her at a Waffle House. "I think she had two full days of freedom and just said, 'I ain't going back.'"

That Sunday, Homan told authorities Marie had fled and left a note for him. "Dear John, I hope you will be able to forgive me....I'm getting ready to leave....It will be best for everybody....We'll be together again.... Please give me an hour to get out of town....Destroy this note." The note reportedly also went on to say that a man named Walter was going to drive her to Atlanta to catch a plane to Canada. There was immediate statewide outrage that Hilley had been granted the release.

"The day the jury found her guilty, John Homan called me with the news that mother was unhappy and felt I had helped convict her. She told him she would get me and my family for putting her in jail," Michael Hilley told the *Anniston Star*. "If she starts to do anything with my family, then I would have no alternative to a physical conflict with my mother. I don't want that because she's my mother." Michael Hilley's fears didn't come to pass. His mother died at 5:06 p.m. on February 26, 1987.

The last time Michael Hilley saw her alive was during a visit to Tutwiler Prison. They "beat around the bushes" on one thousand topics. "I was scared to give her too much information about myself, like where I lived, because I never knew what she would do. It was a lot of guarded speech." As they parted ways, Michael paused. "I started to call her back and ask her very specific questions and not let her lie. I let the moment pass, and I knew it was going to be the last time I saw her alive."

At her funeral, Michael was approached by Homan, who wanted Michael to place in Marie's casket a ceramic swan he said she loved. "I was still angry at him because he had helped her, even if it was in ignorance." Michael wasn't going to put the swan in the coffin, but then he relented. "It wouldn't hurt me to do it, but I knew it would one day cause me a lot of guilt not to."

With Marie in the ground alongside Frank, the Hilley family and all of Alabama were left with questions. People around Marie tended to die, Michael said, yet we may never know how many she killed or injured. Once, Michael asked his mother to help him get a deposit back on an apartment where he had lived in Saks. Marie told him she got the money—though Michael never saw any of it—but added a disturbing fact: the landlord had been killed execution style, hands tied and shot in the head. "I knew something wasn't right there. Why would she tell me that? I never met the guy."

People may forever ask whether Homan was taken in by Hilley's charm or if he knew more about her crimes than he let on. "I always thought he was either the dumbest person who ever lived, or he was deceived by an expert. Maybe it was a combination of the two," Hilley said. "She could be very, very, very persuasive. I think he was a tool she used to get what she wanted, which, at the time, was to get away from being caught." "Calling it bizarre is an understatement," Judge Sam Monk, who presided over the case, told the *Anniston Star*. "I always felt like Homan was as much of a victim as her other husband. She used him. He was gullible. He fell for it."

DeMonia keeps in her attic a letter Homan wrote but never mailed to the Anniston newspaper. "Somehow or another, I think the two of us were destined for each other," Homan wrote of Hilley. "There's so little happiness in the world, and we were both happy. It's hard to walk away from happiness." Homan kept living and working at the Heart of Anniston Inn until he died in 1989 from a shotgun blast to the throat from an irate guest. "She would do anything for me. She fed, clothed and took care of me, as I did her. She consoled me when times were bad and loved me when times were good," Homan wrote. "Marie, I am sad you are gone for my own selfish reasons, but in my heart, I know you are happier wherever you are. Be happy, my love. I love and miss you and always will. Thank you for coming into my life." Despite his devotion to Marie, Homan privately told DeMonia he had himself tested for arsenic exposure. The test came back negative.

"A Lot of Inexplicable Things"

Remembered as charismatic, yet soft-spoken and polite, Marie Hilley was not someone you would expect to commit murder. "She had a charm that was unbelievable. Marie could sell the proverbial refrigerator to an Eskimo," a lifelong friend and childhood sweetheart, Elmer Williamson, told the *Anniston Star*. So how did Marie Hilley come to be one of Alabama's most reviled killers?

"Bottom line? Money. But, at the same time, I think she was always unhappy with her life. I think she always aspired to be something she wasn't, at least in her mind. Money was a way to get there. It didn't matter who she had to hurt or destroy to get there," Michael Hilley said. "She felt unloved as a child," Adcock told the *Anniston Star*. "Her mother and father would leave her with her grandmother for weeks at a time. She felt that her parents, especially her mother, didn't love her."

Hilley's final days are also shrouded in mystery. "She left John, and I don't think he ever saw her again. She had to be somewhere, and the only way she could have done it was with someone helping her," Michael said. There were theories that said she may have been murdered by someone who wanted to keep her quiet forever, DeMonia said. "There were all these stories and suspicions in Anniston that she knew things, she was having affairs and holding things over peoples' heads. There were a lot of inexplicable things there."

Homan, too, had his doubts about how Marie died. "This woman here used to spend entire days in zero-degree weather and knew how to take care of herself and to stay warm. It just doesn't add that she stood in the rain and froze to death," he said. "We had everything going for us. It looked like everything was coming together. I could see the light at the end of the tunnel. I find it hard to believe she would have messed up her world for that."

Unquestionable is the despair and agony Marie Hilley's actions caused. After years of physical therapy, Carol Hilley, her brother said, recovered from being paralyzed, earned a black belt and firefighter's license and retired from the Anniston Army Depot. Today, Michael works as a chaplain in Alabama prisons and teaches. Years ago, Michael received threats from people who said he wrongfully turned in his mother. Carol still lives in the area and still is treated differently to this day, he said. "That's why I have so much admiration for her. I would have packed up and left in two seconds."

Though decades have passed since his mother's crimes, Michael says his life was shaped, in part, by being the son of Anniston's "Black Widow." "It caused me to step up and take more responsibility for myself and the people I care about," Michael said. "It's strange to say, but my life is fuller than it might have been otherwise because it took me down paths I wouldn't have gone down otherwise. I will never consider myself a victim. I think I have worked out most of the things I need to. I don't let it define me." Still, he sometimes thinks of his mother when he looks at his children and grandchildren. "She robbed them of a set of grandparents and great-grandparents."

A funeral director gave Michael a bag that contained the clothes Marie was wearing when she died. He kept it in his garage for years before tossing it out. Once, when he moved, he found the pajamas his father was wearing when he died. "I just threw them out. I think I'm done with letting it have the grip on me that it once did. There's an empty spot there, but it could have been a whole lot worse."

Years ago, Michael Hilley reflected on his life. "I realized I was more like her than I realized. She, at one point, had a heart for people. She would take food to the poor. We got that from her." He also recognized in himself the same self-centered, narcissistic behavior he once saw in Marie Hilley. "It kind of scares me sometimes."

9
JUDITH ANN NEELLEY

The Drain Cleaner Killer

Judith Ann Neelley fired a gun into the back of thirteen-year-old Lisa Ann Millican's head on September 28, 1982, and pushed her off an eighty-foot cliff into Little River Canyon, about ten miles east of Fort Payne. It was the end of three days of torture for the kidnapped teen, but the suffering of Lisa Ann's family and the loved ones of all involved in the senseless, horrific murder continues decades later, with no end in sight.

It all began when Judith Ann was fifteen and living with her mother, who Neelley said was a heavy drinker and brought many men to their rundown Murfreesboro trailer. Her alcoholic father died in a motorcycle wreck when she was nine years old. She has said that some of the men who visited her mother pushed aside the thin sheet that was her bedroom door, and she fought to keep them off her.

Then she met Alvin Neelley, a twenty-six-year-old married car thief who won her over with his "flashy smile and bright eyes." Alvin was, she later testified, "one of the last romantics." Alvin convinced teenage Judith Ann to run away to Georgia. It seemed like a great adventure with a man who treated her like an adult, Judith Ann testified. The two called each other Boney and Claude, a pun on the outlaw couple Bonnie and Clyde.

Soon, Judith Ann later said, the violent, jealous, Bible-reading Alvin was beating her, chaining her to bedposts, making her sleep naked on motel floors and assaulting her with a toilet plunger and baseball bat. "He promised that there was no place he couldn't find me and that if he couldn't find me, he would start killing members of my family until I showed up," Judith Ann

Judith Ann Neelley smiles as she is escorted into court in 1983. *Courtesy of the Alabama Department of Archives and History, donated by Alabama Media Group.*

said. "I wasn't a person; I was just a piece of meat to him." The wife Alvin left for Judith Ann later said he had turned her into a slave during their five years together.

Judith Ann, however, seemed to be an eager participant in their crime spree. While pregnant with twins, Judith Ann often held a .38-caliber pistol while they pulled several stickups—until the two were busted. She gave birth to a boy and girl in 1980, while she was incarcerated at the Regional Youth Development Center in Rome, Georgia. While at the juvenile facility, Judith Ann developed a hatred of the employees, just as Alvin's hatred of those he felt wronged him grew. In a letter to her from his Georgia prison cell, Alvin vowed, "Everyone who has made me unhappy, the rest of their lives will be unhappy and destroyed....I may smile, but on the inside, I want to destroy and if I can, I will."

Soon after they were released and reunited, Judith Ann was pregnant again. While the twins stayed with a relative, the couple escalated their crimes. Alvin remained jealous of her, Judith Ann said, following her into restrooms and ordering her to stay away from the windows of their motel rooms. Alvin Neelley later denied claims he abused Judith Ann and said she chose to murder to hide her involvement in a prostitution and pornography ring. "Her explanation was that she enjoyed being able to make people do what she wanted," an AP report quoted him as saying. Alvin said he went along with the crimes out of fear she would report him for violating parole on a grand larceny charge. He claimed Judith Ann only let him live so she could pin the crimes on him.

Juvenile case workers in Rome and Macon, Georgia, soon began receiving threatening phone calls. A bullet was fired into the window of the home of Regional Youth Development employee Ken Dooley on September 12, 1982. The next night, Linda Adair, another employee of the center, had a Molotov cocktail thrown at her house. A woman then called Adair and the Floyd County, Georgia police to say she threw the bomb because she was angry about her treatment at the center two years earlier, according to Chief Jim Free. "You both will die before the night's over," the caller told Adair of her and Dooley. "For the abuse I took, they are both going to die," the caller told police. Though she didn't give her name, the officer who took the call memorized her voice, something that would become a crucial piece of evidence weeks later.

"I Gave Her a Shot in the Neck"

Lisa Ann, a resident of the Ethel Harpst Home for Juveniles in Cedartown, was playing video games in the Aladdin's Castle Arcade at Rome's Riverbend Mall on September 25, 1982. Judith Ann saw Lisa Ann and thought the girl looked like the character Joanie Cunningham from the TV show *Happy Days*. The two started talking, and Lisa Ann left with Neelley to be delivered to Alvin. It was the beginning of three days of agony for Lisa Ann.

Judith Ann's young twins were back with her and Alvin, watching cartoons as Lisa Ann was chained naked to the foot of the bed in room 12 of the Five Points Motel in Scottsboro. "With Lisa, my brother and I were there," their daughter, April Neelley, told a reporter years later. "We probably played together." Alvin raped the girl repeatedly, and Judith Ann later said she began to fear that if Lisa Ann were freed, they would both end up back in youth homes. "Mrs. Neelley said she would get into trouble and Lisa was better dead than in a youth detention center," DeKalb County district attorney investigator Danny Smith later testified.

Three days after coaxing her out of an arcade, Judith Ann was handcuffing Lisa Ann to a tree. "She asked me to let her go. She said she wouldn't tell

Lisa Ann Millican (*right in both photographs*) with her siblings. *Contributed by Cassie Millican.*

anybody if I just let her go or take her to the Harpst home or her mother's," Judith Ann later testified. "I told her I'd give her a shot and put her to sleep, and we'd be gone. I got out a syringe from my pocketbook and walked over to where Lisa was at. I was just looking at her, and Al hollered and told me to do it. So, I gave her a shot in the neck." She testified that their twins were sleeping nearby in a car while the young mother injected Lisa Ann with Liquid Plumber and Drano.

Alvin had supposedly heard a jailhouse myth that drain cleaner was an indetectable means of committing murder. The first injection "didn't do anything" to Lisa Ann, testified Judith Ann, so she injected her again on the other side of her neck. The child complained the injections hurt. "I told her to hold on." She gave her two more—one in each arm and two in the rear. Alvin cursed at Judith Ann to "do it right" then told her to shoot her, Judith Ann testified. "I was holding the gun....I couldn't pull the trigger," Judith Ann testified. "Al hollered....'Do it, bitch.'...I pulled the trigger." Lisa Ann fell backward, getting blood on Judith Ann's jeans. She pushed Millican off the cliff and tossed the syringes and bloody jeans down behind Lisa Ann. Judith Ann changed her clothes, and the family went for breakfast.

Judith Ann's defense attorney later asked why she didn't shoot Alvin instead of Lisa Ann. "He didn't tell me to." She was also challenged by a prosecutor: "Suppose he told you to put the gun up to your temple, cock the hammer and pull the trigger—would you have done it?" "Yes sir," Judith

Ann replied as the audience sniggered. It was later revealed that Judith Ann had approached several other girls hoping to lure them for the same torture that filled the final days of Lisa Ann's short life.

"Night Rider and Lady Sundown"

Soon after Lisa Ann's murder, someone described as sounding like a "Southern country White woman" called the Dekalb County, Alabama sheriff's office five times, as well as a radio station and the police in Rome, Georgia. The caller said a body was in a canyon and that she was the one who put it there.

That night, lawmen searched by flashlight and found Lisa Ann's crumpled body by a tree with multiple syringes nearby. A pair of bloody jeans was hanging from a branch. "That's how we found her," Dekalb County chief deputy Cecil Reed said at the time. Ropes were used to recover Lisa Ann's body the next day. "I think she's a smart person and one who is playing games with us. If she hadn't made it a point to call us, we probably never would have found [Lisa Ann]," said Dekalb County sheriff Harold Richards.

One of the calls was heard by a police officer, who recognized the voice as the woman who called about the attacks on the homes of the Rome youth workers weeks earlier. Five days after Lisa Ann's murder, a woman matching Judith Ann's description offered a ride to Debbie Smith, thirteen, of Rome. Debbie declined.

That same day, John Hancock and his fiancé, Janice Kay Chatman, were stopped by Judith Ann, who asked them for directions. Hancock said Judith claimed she did not understand the directions, so the couple got in the car with her. She got on a CB radio with Alvin, whom she called "Night Rider." She went by the handle "Lady Sundown." They all ended up meeting at a restaurant. "Alvin Neelley decided that he wanted me to go with him and Kay to go with Judith Ann Neelley because the twins, their children, were with them," Hancock told WZDK-TV. They eventually stopped on a dirt road, where Hancock went to urinate. Judith Ann followed him with a gun.

"If we're going to do it, we better get it over with," Hancock later said Alvin called out to Judith. Hancock tried to talk to her, but she told him to walk with his back turned. "Get it over with," Alvin yelled. "Don't worry about your girlfriend," Judith Ann told Hancock. "I'll take care of her, too." Hancock, then twenty-six, shifted his body a half-inch as Judith shot him from behind. He told the TV station that it was something he remembered from his military training and may have saved his life as the bullet pierced his body.

Janice Kay wasn't as fortunate. She was taken to the couple's motel room, tortured and raped before she was taken to a remote area and shot. "When Judith Ann Neelley shot Janice Kay in the back, it did not kill her. Alvin Neelley grabbed up Janice Kay and put her against a tree, and Judith Ann walked right up and point blank to her chest, shot her again and ended her life," Hancock told the station.

Hancock crawled to the road and was found by a trucker; he was then taken to a hospital, where the bullet was removed. Judith Ann and Alvin, meanwhile, had kidnapped a young girl from Nashville and taken her to a Murfreesboro motel, where they kept her naked and chained to a sink.

Released from the hospital and sitting on a bench at the Rome Police Station, Hancock heard a recording an investigator was playing for Debbie Smith. "Y'all looking for Lisa Ann Millican, on the run from the Harpst home," the voice asked. Hancock barged into the room and said that was the voice of the woman who shot him. Hancock described the Neelleys' vehicles to police.

In October 1982, Judith Ann was arrested at Murfreesboro's University Inn on bad check charges. When Alvin found out about the arrest, he freed the Nashville abduction victim. Alvin visited Judith Ann in jail until police tried to arrest him on bad check charges. When a woman who said she was Judith Ann's mother went into the jail to post bail, an officer grew suspicious and walked to the parking lot and found Alvin in a red Ford Granada.

Both in custody, the couple soon led police to Janice Kay's body. In the couple's cars, police found two rifles and three handguns, including a .38-caliber pistol. Police immediately began to wonder if the couple was linked to other murders.

Chattooga County, Georgia sheriff Gary McConnell, at the time, said Alvin claimed to have information about nine murders in Alabama and Georgia, and the victims could be found near Dothan, Opelika and DeKalb Counties in Alabama and Macon, Albany, Columbus and Gordon Counties in Georgia. Alvin didn't exactly confess. "He knew how they were found, how the women were killed, and he knew what these other people looked like," McConnell said. "He is familiar with these cases down to the last detail."

"Heinous, Atrocious, and Cruel"

As Judith Ann and Alvin's crimes came to light, people across the South were outraged. "You go messing with little girls, you get my dander up," said Floyd Michael Patterson, a mechanic who watched as police retrieved a car from a canyon as possible evidence. "If somebody did that to my kids and they caught them, the law wouldn't have time enough to do something to them." The retrieved car was apparently not connected to the murders.

With her trial nearing, Judith Ann, on January 3, 1983, gave birth to a boy. The child was taken in by her family. Plans were made to sequester the jury at DeSoto State Park. Defense attorney Bob French told the jury that, at Alvin's hands, Judith Ann was "reduced to an animal, an instrument. She was an extension of a man who perceived himself as Clyde Barrow and of his women as Bonnie Parker." French said because Alvin was convinced Judith was cheating, he made her bring him female victims. DeKalb County district attorney Richard Igou waved off Judith's plea of insanity. "Under law, this defense does not include abnormal behavior manifested by repeated criminal and antisocial acts. And what has happened here is a criminal, antisocial act of the highest degree."

"I hope people will understand when my trial is over," Judith Ann said during the trial. "They will never understand it all, but I hope they understand it enough." She cried in court when Lisa Ann's blood-soaked blouse was entered into evidence. Hairs found on Lisa Ann's blouse were "microscopically similar" to Judith Ann's, a state forensic scientist testified. Judith Ann took the stand in her own defense. "I was too scared of him to ask him why he wanted anything done. I just did it.…I'd do whatever he told me to do."

Alvin's attorney, Brit Miller, in preparing for the Chatman murder trial, watched Judith Ann's testimony and told reporters it was Judith Ann who was the mastermind. "I don't think Alvin had the mental capacity to be as scheming and cunning as they're making him out to be." When Igou asked Judith Ann if Alvin was a "vicious animal," she replied, "He needs help. Alvin has mental problems and needs help." She denied orchestrating the murders. The prosecution read to the jury an unmailed letter she had written Alvin in jail, saying she would love him until death. She wrote that she expected to be in jail a long time and asked that he not forget her. Although he admitted to being "biased and prejudiced" against Judith Ann, Dr. Alexander Salillas of the state department of mental health said Judith Ann was sane at the time of Lisa Ann's murder. Deputy district atttorney Mike O'Dell said Lisa Ann was supposed to be on a "fun outing, but it turned into a living hell."

In his closing arguments, French pleaded for mercy. "Judith Neelley is not a killer. She has bruises on her brain. She can't formulate a thought. We can't show you the bruises on the inside….She's been trained like an animal trainer would train a puppy to be a vicious dog." Life behind bars for Judith Ann, French said, would be justice for Lisa Ann. "You'll never have to worry about her committing another crime. She will be locked away in a world where the walls clang, and there's a constant musty smell, and you never see the light of day." Judith Ann was, he said, "a misbegotten child of the times" and compared her to the "Bride of Frankenstein."

"She knew what she was doing, she knew it was wrong," Igou countered. "Alvin was to use and abuse her sexually, and Judith was to kill her." It was, he said, "one of the most bizarre reigns of terror ever seen in Alabama and Georgia….What we have failed to see from this defendant is any remorse."

During a trial break, Judith Ann told reporters she had developed an admiration for Patricia Hearst, the heiress who was kidnapped in California by a left-wing organization in 1974 and went on to commit robberies with the group. "I never really thought much about Patricia Hearst until this happened to me….I remember reading about it, but now I understand what she went through."

The jury deliberated for three hours and forty-five minutes before convicting Judith Ann of capital murder on March 22, 1983; ten of the jurors recommended life without parole, two wanted execution. Alabama law at the time, however, allowed the judge to override the jury's recommendation and order execution. Judge Randall Cole did just that, calling the crime "heinous, atrocious, and cruel."

"I don't want to die. There's so much I can do to help. I just want to prove it. I don't belong in the electric chair," Judith Ann told the judge. In 2017, Alabama became the last state in America to abolish judicial override.

"I Wanted Her to Get the Death Penalty"

Judith Ann, then eighteen, was taken to prison on April 18, 1983. She was the youngest person to ever be sentenced to die in the electric chair in Alabama, and she was the youngest woman ever sentenced to die in America. Four days later, John Louis Evans III became the first person to be executed in

Judith Ann Neelley in a 1984 prison interview. *Courtesy of the Alabama Department of Archives and History, donated by Alabama Media Group.*

Alabama since the U.S. Supreme Court reinstated the death penalty in 1976, eighteen years prior. Evans had been convicted in the 1977 murder of a Mobile pawn shop owner. During the execution, an electrode exploded, and Evans was burned. It took fourteen minutes to finish the execution. "I won't think about getting executed because I hope I don't," Judith told *UPI*. "I don't ask God for me not to be electrocuted. I just ask that if I'm going to be electrocuted, give me the strength to go through it."

Neelley told the wire service she was frequently shackled by guards and stared at by other Tutwiler inmates. "What has me so angry is the way I was treated. Everyone is treated at least half human. I was treated worse than an animal." Prison spokesman Ron Tate defended the measures. "She's a young girl who injected a thirteen-year-old child with Drano. Someone who has been convicted of a crime of that nature bears watching."

Judith Ann said she would never lose hope of being free. "I feel like there is a purpose for me in this world, and it isn't to die in the electric chair….I've got my trust in the Lord, and I've got to do what he needs for me to do," Judith Ann told the *Alabama Journal* in 1984. If freed, she said she would like to work with battered women and children.

Her attorney, Bob French, said that though he had grown close to Judith Ann, the case "was a born loser," impossible to win because of the visceral reaction conjured by Lisa Ann's death. "Every person I know has put Drano in a drain once in his life," French told AP. The father of twins himself, French received hate mail for defending her; one of his staffers had a mail carrier tell them Judith Ann should "fry." French said he was often asked what he would do if a child of his was murdered. "I would like to say I'd be forgiving, that I would let the system work, and I would not take revenge on my own," he said. "I know that lurking in my capabilities lies a killer, and it might be different if it were my own daughter."

A year after the conviction, French said his income had plummeted; two associates left his practice, and he had laid off a secretary and an investigator. His reputation hurt by a rumor of a jailhouse affair with Judith Ann and anger that he had defended her, French was no longer the swaggering lawyer who cruised Decatur in a Rolls Royce or buzzed the city in his own jet. "I've had 50 years practice being obnoxious. It's just so difficult to stop," he told AP. "I wanted her to get the death penalty," French told AP. "Every time I looked at Judy, I was seeing a murderer and wondering how in the world could she do it."

Still, French came to see her as "a little girl" and called her "my baby." He told reporters she had not confided in him the extent of the abuse until she took the stand. Had French known, he said he would have pushed to move the trial to Birmingham and gotten more Black women on the jury. They wouldn't have convicted. "They have seen it. Their husbands are out fighting in the White man's world all day. They come home tired and frustrated and take it out on their wives….They understand it."

French, in 2017, released a book, *Beaten, Battered, and Damned: The Drano Murder Trial*. In the book, he confirmed that Judith Ann did not receive any money from its publication. "I gave that woman the best defense a person could give," French told me. "Judith Neelley cost me $340,000 out of pocket. I don't owe her a damn thing. I went bankrupt defending her, and every cent I get off the book goes into my pocket. I laugh all the way to the bank."

Lisa Ann's sister-in-law, Cassie Millican, said she joined forces with a victim's rights group in Alabama, and in 2019, after years of pleading from the family, Alabama passed "Lisa's Law," which prevents convicted killers from profiting off of crime through books, movies or other entertainment. Cassie shared with me a letter she said Judith Ann wrote from prison. Neelley said French was constantly arranging interviews for her after her arrest and conviction. "I was naïve, believing him when he said we were doing it to help other battered women to enlighten people about physical abuse." Judith Ann said she only later learned, once he was no longer her lawyer, that he was being paid for the interviews. The letter states she no longer gives interviews; I attempted to write to her but received no reply. "I promise I never received one cent. Would not have taken any nor given the interviews had I known. My sole intent was to help other battered women. I am terribly ashamed," states the letter Cassie shared.

French considers Cassie an opportunist and Lisa's Law unconstitutional. Even if it was constitutional, French told me it did not apply to him because the book was about him, not Judith. Lisa Ann's family says they will never stop fighting to keep Judith Ann in prison and fighting to defend Lisa Ann in death in a way they couldn't in life. "She never got to experience the love of that first crush," Cassie told me. "She never got to find herself or become a mother of her own. These were the things cruelly snatched from her. She was her mother's baby, and she just wanted to go home. She was taunted with being back in her mother's arms until the bitter, disgusting end."

"ALABAMA'S VERSION OF CHARLIE MANSON"

Judith Ann awaited execution until Governor Fob James, in one of his last acts in office in January 1999, commuted her sentence to life, just as prosecutors were trying to nail down an execution date. "That DeKalb County jury, which heard all of the facts of that heinous crime in the months right after the events took place, convicted her to life in prison," James told the *Cherokee County Post* in 2002. "Then the judge changed the sentence to death.…To kill her would not be justice."

Weeks after the commutation, then–Alabama attorney general Bill Pryor, now a federal judge who has been mentioned as a nominee for the U.S. Supreme Court, said that the decision meant Judith Ann would be eligible for parole in fifteen years. "When I commuted that sentence, I thought—and my lawyers had investigated it—that there could be no possibility of parole," James told the *Cherokee County Post*. "It is a total contradiction to commute a death sentence and then allow for the possibility of parole."

Birmingham Post-Herald columnist Ted Bryant, in 1998, had speculated what James would do if Neelley became the first woman in Alabama to be executed since Rhonda Bell Martin in 1957. "The specter of Karla Faye Tucker and Judith Ann Neelley seemed to be in the room....After much agonizing over her changed life in prison, Texas put Tucker to death by lethal injection last week for the pickax murders of a man and a woman in the 1980s. Texas Gov. George Bush refused to grant a stay," Bryant wrote. "What would James have done in that case? 'That's a tough one,' James said, for once apparently unsure of what he would do." A former James aide told www.AL.com that James did not want to wake one day to read that a woman he had the power to save had been put to death.

The commutation sparked outrage. "She told us how she and her husband tortured little Lisa before finally putting her to death. She showed no emotion, no remorse, no sadness," O'Dell told the *Cherokee County Post*. "[James] did this without speaking to [the DA's office] or asking our opinion. It is clear he did not want us to be involved in his decision."

The decision, however, was welcomed by Judith's daughter April, who was said to have been in the car when Lisa Ann was killed, according to a post she wrote on Facebook in 2014. In 1999, before the commutation, Judith Ann called April and told her through tears that her final appeal had been denied. April sent the governor a poem and asked that James help her and her brother to "have a happy ending." "God bless Fob James for doing just that," April wrote. "Though we are still fighting for a truly happy ending, you gave us the chance at it....Our rage and anger over the evil [James] unleashed on our family will never end. To this day, he's never offered a single apology. A single phone call," Lisa's sister-in-law wrote in an email to me. "Abominable! He's a spineless coward in our eyes, and I hope his name forever brings shame for what he's done. His legacy is tainted with Shame!"

The legislature changed state law in 2003, specifically to block Neelley from the possibility of parole. On October 21, 2005, Alvin died at Oconee Regional Medical Center. He was fifty-two. "We're not going to build a

Judith Ann Neelley in the state's most recently posted mugshot. *Courtesy of the Alabama Department of Corrections.*

shrine for him," Judith Ann's brother Bill Adams said. "They were married to each other, so there's a little sadness there," said Judith Ann's ex-sister-in-law, Kathy Bauguess. In 2009, April Neelley, one of the twins born to Alvin and Judith Ann, told the *Rome News-Tribune* that Alvin had a stroke or heart attack and fell into a coma after surgery. She said she and her sister decided to remove him from life support. "We both made our peace with him," April said. "I had a letter I had written him that I never sent, asking him to please tell the truth about what happened all those years ago." Alvin Neelley was buried in a prison cemetery in Statesboro, Georgia.

When the fifteen-year waiting period for parole ended in 2014, Neelley filed a federal lawsuit challenging the law that Alabama legislators had drafted specifically to keep her in prison forever. A judge ruled the law was unconstitutional, and she appeared before the parole board on May 23, 2018. "The first thing I said to all of my friends is you have got to be kidding," Hancock told WZDK-TV of the moment he found out about the parole hearing. "How can a convicted murderer be commuted to life and then be allowed parole? That's like giving someone a loaded gun and telling them go out and kill as many people as you want.… Everybody needs to know what kind of a monster that woman really is. If I compared her to anyone, she would be Alabama's version of Charlie Manson," Hancock told the station.

Judith Ann had asked to waive her right to a hearing and said she wanted to appear before the board years down the road. But she was told it was now or never. Lisa Ann's family planned to fight to keep her killer behind bars, asking people to write to the parole board.

"SHE JUST NEEDS TO DO HER TIME"

"Under no circumstances should Judith Ann Neelley be granted parole. Her crimes…include acts of unspeakable brutality. And her character includes a disturbing tendency to manipulate others toward her own, violent ends,"

Governor Kay Ivey, Alabama's second ever female governor, said before the hearing. Ivey said she would not have commuted the sentence. "Do not forget the depravity of Ms. Neelley's crimes. Do not forget the danger Ms. Neelley poses to society."

O'Dell told the board, according to www.AL.com, "I've probably prosecuted over 200 murder defendants. I have never prosecuted one other defendant who murdered for sheer sport. She loved killing.…If anyone in the history of Alabama ever deserved to be executed, it was Judith Ann Neelley."

"That took a part of my life away," Lisa Ann's brother, Calvin Millican, said. "And it took Lisa's whole life away. She's no longer here….Judith Ann Neelley is a very cruel, sick person."

The board refused to grant parole.

"It just tears me up every time something comes up and the possibility of her getting parole is just terribly wrong," Calvin told my longtime friend and colleague Mike Cason after the hearing. "It upsets me. It just needs to stop. She just needs to do her time here." Neelley will not be eligible for parole again until 2023. Calvin said he will be there to oppose the parole yet again.

Even if Judith Ann is granted parole in Alabama, she will likely be sent to a Georgia prison for the attack on John Hancock and Janice Chatman. Montgomery attorney Julian McPhillips was one of those who fought at the hearing for Neelley, whom he had known for twenty years, and urged the board to grant parole. "We're seeking not so much a parole as a transfer. A transfer to Georgia. Because everybody knows she's on a life sentence over there."

McPhillips and O'Dell disagreed on the claim that Alvin had brainwashed Judith. "To say that Ms. Neelley was brainwashed is a vast understatement. She was more like a zombie, no independent mind, no rational mind of her own, coerced by her husband," McPhillips said. "The whole concept of brainwashing and under the influence of Alvin Neelley was debunked at trial," O'Dell said. "To say today that she was under the influence of somebody else and is still not willing to take responsibility for the acts is unimaginable to me."

Kenneth Brothers told the board he got to know Neelley because of her participation in weekly small prison ministry meetings. "Her desire is that God would use her wherever or however he wants," Brothers told the board.

"SHE JUST WANTED TO GO HOME"

As Lisa Ann's family carries their decades of grief and prepares to fight the next parole hearing, Judith's daughter April, who slept in the car as a two-year-old as her mother killed Millican, has pleaded for mercy for her mother. "She said Dad held a gun on my brother and me at one point and threatened if she didn't do as he said, he would kill us. Why wouldn't she believe him?" April Neeley told the *Rome News-Tribune*. "She made choices that a lot of people wouldn't have made, but she was a victim herself, whether anyone believes it or not. She chose her children over complete strangers, and that's what it boils down to," April said then. She said she and her twin brother were raised by Alvin's mother. "In the beginning, my father and I had a great relationship," April told the newspaper. "I didn't know about the ultimatums he had given my mother until after I formed a relationship with him. But after I found out, I stopped going to see him."

In 2014, April posted a public plea on Facebook for mercy for her mother, saying her father held a gun on her and her brother as he demanded Judith Ann kill Lisa Ann. "Years of physical and mental abuse, months of sleep and food deprivation, she fully believed his threat and fell for his trick," April wrote. Her father, she believes, wanted her mother to pull the trigger to keep evidence from pointing at him. "She chose my life and my brother's life over Lisa's life and over Janice Chatman's life."

April did not celebrate her thirteenth birthday, knowing Lisa never got to celebrate her fourteenth birthday. April has also written that freeing her mother would not do a disservice to the memories of Lisa Ann and Janice. But Lisa Ann's family doesn't see things the same way.

"She was vulnerable, but she was tough. She was raised with a lot of male cousins, so she was tough when she needed to be, but she was gentle souled, she was shy, and she was loving. A mama's baby who wore out the song "Playing with the Queen of Hearts" like it was no one's business," Cassie Millican wrote to me. "There was a four-year age difference between her brother, Calvin, and herself, so being close in age, they had their squabbles. He often tells the story of cutting all the hair off her dolls, where she, in return, told him to scrape a plate of food he didn't like out the window and told on him," Cassie recalled. When their third sibling, Tina, was born, Lisa "thought that was her baby." "Lisa just had turned 13. The tender-hearted tomboy was growing up. She developed her first crush and was beginning to discover and find herself," Cassie wrote.

Family members of Lisa Ann have turned on their television and, without warning, seen a dramatic reenactment of her murder, Cassie told me. "No one asks our permission, and people are just now beginning to show respect since we've fought back. People fail to see that a child whose been in her grave longer than she lived on this Earth was a human being with hopes and dreams."

10

BETTY WILSON

Huntsville's Twin Sister Doctor Killer

Peggy Lowe sang with the First Baptist Church of Vincent choir days after a Montgomery jury spared the Shelby County first-grade teacher from execution or life in an Alabama prison. "I wasn't the only one who faced the death penalty," Peggy told her church supporters that Sunday. "We all face the death penalty by the way we live. We die by the way we live." When Peggy was acquitted on September 22, 1993, a supporter yelled into a hallway courthouse payphone, "Praise God, she's innocent!"

Peggy's twin sister, Betty Wilson, at the time, was still adjusting to life in Tutwiler Prison with no hope for parole after her March 3, 1993 conviction for what Tuscaloosa jurors agreed was the 1992 murder-for-hire of Betty's husband of fourteen years. Betty was also filing a lawsuit on her own behalf, claiming a fellow prison inmate had thrown urine into her cell, and she sought $20,000 from the state for "mental and emotional abuse."

The Shelby County Board of Education voted 4–0 soon after her acquittal to return Peggy to a Vincent Elementary School classroom, despite protests from some parents.

The Alabama Supreme Court voted 4–1 to deny Betty a new trial, with only one justice—former governor John Patterson—arguing that prosecutors had failed to adequately substantiate the testimony of James Dennison White, a handyman at Peggy's school, who pleaded guilty to the brutal May 22, 1992 beating and stabbing death of Huntsville ophthalmologist Dr. Jack Wilson. Prosecutors claimed that White had agreed to kill the doctor for $5,000. White agreed to testify against the sisters in exchange for being allowed to plead guilty to murder with a sentence of life in prison with a chance of parole.

More than twenty-eight years after the murder of Dr. Wilson shocked Alabama and grabbed the attention of national tabloids and TV producers, questions still surround the case and the outcome of the two trials. Dr. Wilson's family, friends and colleagues still face the void that was created when they were robbed of the man who wore Christmas neckties in the summer, cared for patients who couldn't pay, snored through operas, treated staff members like family and ate his peanut butter straight from the jar.

And while one twin sister walks free, the other faces the likelihood of dying in prison. "There's an innocent woman in prison this morning. I hope you will pray that the decision will be reversed," Peggy said that Sunday after her acquittal. "Faith is the key that unlocks the door."

After the state supreme court's decision, it seemed no amount of faith would unlock the prison doors for Betty Wilson. Her numerous affairs, including one with a Black man (something that was still widely looked down on in Alabama at the time); her comments about wanting to be a wealthy widow rather than divorce her seriously ill husband; and the fact that she was in a recovery group for alcoholics was all used to brand Betty with a scarlet "A" at her own trial and, later, at Peggy's trial.

Betty told *Birmingham Post-Herald* journalist Elaine Witt in 2005 that it was impossible for her to defend herself against such claims. "You know, where a man is assertive, a woman is a bitch, where a man is free to do his own thing, a woman is a slut, and never mind what has gone on. What was between my husband and me was our business….It's been made like we were the only couple in the world who allowed each other freedom, and that was something that Jack insisted on….I was convicted because of human nature being such that we enjoy pointing our finger, not in purity but in piety," Betty said then. "I'm not being critical of my jury. I think that they're just being human and fell into the trap that was designed for them, and, unfortunately, we didn't defend it."

"I Love My Mother"

The Wilson twins were born on July 14, 1945, two of four sisters, and graduated from Gadsden High School in 1964. Betty was a student council officer, pep club member and was in plays and talent shows, while Peggy

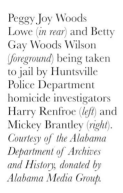

Peggy Joy Woods Lowe (*in rear*) and Betty Gay Woods Wilson (*foreground*) being taken to jail by Huntsville Police Department homicide investigators Harry Renfroe (*left*) and Mickey Brantley (*right*). *Courtesy of the Alabama Department of Archives and History, donated by Alabama Media Group.*

was a homecoming queen and beauty contest winner. Both were married right out of high school and both were divorced after about five years. Betty married Dr. Wilson after meeting him at a Huntsville hospital where she worked as a dialysis nurse. Peggy married music teacher and minister Wayne Lowe.

On the night he was murdered, Dr. Wilson was seen by a neighbor using a baseball bat to drive a candidate's campaign sign into their yard on Boulder Circle in southeast Huntsville. The 130-pound fifty-five-year-old who suffered lasting effects from a surgery for Crohn's disease then went back inside. Betty returned from a meeting for alcoholics in recovery when she found her husband dead in a pool of blood, a baseball bat lying beside him. He had been severely beaten, with wounds to his head, arms and hands, and he was stabbed twice in the chest. Betty ran to a neighbor's house and called 911. That neighbor, Donald Seija, said Betty was "obviously upset."

The couple had planned a trip to Santa Fe, New Mexico, for the next day when Betty found Dr. Wilson dead in their home that Friday night. Instead, Betty was arrested for capital murder less than a week later, along with Lowe and White. Then–Huntsville police chief Ric Ottman said the forty-seven-year-old twins paid White, then forty-one, to kill Dr. Wilson. The arrests came after White bragged about killing someone over the weekend in Huntsville, said then–Shelby County sheriff James Jones.

The killing and arrests stunned people in Huntsville and Shelby Counties. "As far as I know, she was a good person," said Calvin Smith, who was one of several deacons who put up $300,000 in property to post Peggy's bond.

Smith was also the principal at Vincent Elementary. "I love my mother, and I hope the charges against her aren't true, and that's about all my attorney will let me say," Betty's son, Dink Taylor, said in 1992.

"Those Girls Weren't Raised that Way"

Investigators were initially tight-lipped about the case, but as Betty's trial neared, allegations were revealed that drew the eyes of America to Alabama and painted a sordid picture of greed, betrayal and manipulation that culminated in the vicious killing of a beloved doctor.

"I was trying to win [Lowe's] love and affection," White stated in a taped confession that was played at a June 1992 hearing. "It started as a joke.… She kept calling and pushing me to get something done to help her sister." White said that weeks before the murder, $2,500 was passed to him, which he quickly spent to clear overdraft fees at a local bank, pay off bad checks that he had written to a grocery store and to help his children.

"I will try to keep him off death row. If I can do that, I will have won this case—or at least done a good job," White's court-appointed defender, Roy Miller, said at the time. I spoke to White by phone from the Red Eagle Work Center. "Yeah, I done it," White said when asked if he killed the doctor. "I hate that I done it. I wish I could apologize to his sons for taking their dad." However, White said Peggy convinced him that he would be killing an "abusive man, a mean man" and not a pillar of the community. "The one who should have got the time was Peggy Lowe," White told me. It must be noted that White has changed his story over the years, confessing, recanting, walking back from recanting—saying, at times, Betty gave him instructions and then saying he never interacted with her. "I don't know Betty Wilson; I know Peggy Lowe. Whether Betty talked Peggy into talking to me or gave Peggy money to give me, I don't know. Betty never said anything to me," White told me.

At the time, observers across the state and nation were impatient to find out exactly what led to the cruel death of Dr. Jack Wilson. In 1992, television networks looked to hastily produce a made-for-TV movie about the murder, even as the trial was in its earliest stages. People wanted to know everything about the twin sisters who were at the center of the doctor's alleged murder-for-hire-trial. "Those girls weren't raised that way," Wayne Lowe said, according to AP. "All I know is when Betty saw it, she could hardly talk.

James Dennison White in the mugshot most recently posted by the Alabama Department of Corrections. *Courtesy of the Alabama Department of Corrections.*

She was in shock, and she was just in a daze, all through the funeral."

The case began to have a ripple effect across life and politics in Huntsville. After a Huntsville homicide investigator testified that one of the many men Betty had affairs with was a Black man, the man quit his job as a risk management officer for Huntsville, although he said the move had nothing to do with the testimony. And while Betty was being depicted as money-hungry, sex-crazed and murderous, Peggy's friends rallied around her. "Those of us who know her have never seen any evidence of any action that would indicate any bad intent," said Reverend H.L. Martin, according to AP. "All we know is what she's done for people who are down." Martin said Peggy took in those in need, like a young pregnant girl who was thrown out of her house. "Even if she told me she was involved in this, I wouldn't believe her," said friend Lallouise McGraw, eighty-six. "She would have to be a Jekyll/Hyde personality." Georganna Ritch took over Peggy's class after the arrest. "I'd come in and watch her teach class on her breaks, and her students would always cling to her."

Dr. Wilson's three sons were battling a last will that placed Betty as the executor of her dead husband's $6.3 million estate, arguing that he had a new will in the works when he died.

In a letter to the *Huntsville Times*, Madison County district attorney Mo Brooks apologized for saying Betty was campaigning for opponent Tim Morgan the day Dr. Wilson was killed. Morgan accepted the apology and said the doctor had long been a friend and a supporter. Brooks lost that election to Morgan, yet he maintained his reputation for eyebrow-raising statements long after he was elected in 2010 to represent the area in Congress.

With nine companies competing for the rights to the story, Wilson's three sons selected producer Larry Thompson to make a movie for CBS, tentatively called *Black Widows: The Alabama Twins Murder*. Thompson was operating under the assumption that one or both sisters was guilty. "Our story would certainly only be viable in the situation that we had a conviction, but we had to get started on production," Thompson said, according to AP. "What I want to do is a sensitive, accurate approach about twins and a small Alabama town. I think the family members felt that maybe I had a feel for that." The made-for-TV-movie *Separated by Murder* premiered on CBS on April 12, 1994, and starred Sharon Gless of *Cagney & Lacey* fame as Memphis twins Holly Fay Walker and Lily Mae Stokely.

"It Doesn't Bring Him Back"

At Betty's trial, her attorneys, Marc Sandlin and Bobby Lee Cook, said to be the inspiration for Andy Griffith's folksy Georgia lawyer *Matlock*, faced a monumental obstacle—Betty's reputation. Sandlin said Betty had a shot if the jury could "get over Betty's lifestyle." Limestone district attorney James Fry said Betty was "a selfish woman, obsessed with her own appearance and having things," including a Mercedes and BMW. "Though it appeared she had everything, she wanted more. And not just more, she wanted it all, and she wanted it now."

Prosecutors pieced together a timeline leading to Dr. Wilson's murder. White testified that he and Peggy had sex on May 15, 1992, and she began pressuring him, saying if the murder was not committed soon, she would have to repay her sister the $2,500 that had been given to White back in April. With that money already spent, White told Peggy he would need traveling money to go to Huntsville to kill Dr. Wilson. Acting on what White says were Peggy's instructions, he found $200 in a Huntsville library book, *Sleeping Beauty and the Firebird*, at Guntersville State Park, where Betty was attending a retreat for recovering alcoholics. The book was supposed to be waiting for White in Betty's unlocked BMW; however, a Guntersville park guard would not let White enter, so the book was delivered to White, at Betty's request, outside the park.

After he left the park, White testified that he purchased two packs of cigarettes and a case of beer, which he used to wash down fifteen caffeine tablets known as "fast ones." Using directions, which he again said Peggy gave him, White then drove to Wilson's house. Parked in the driveway was a blue truck that belonged to one of the Wilsons' sons. Following what he again said were Peggy's directions, White left and didn't carry out the killing with family around.

Returning home to Vincent, White testified that he received a call from Betty wanting to know why it was taking him so long to get rid of her husband. White claimed Peggy also called him to say that Dr. Wilson had to

Lawyers Marc Sandlin and Charlie Hooper with their client Betty Wilson. *Courtesy of the Alabama Department of Archives and History, donated by Alabama Media Group.*

be killed before May 24, as Betty did not want to spend the night in a New Mexico hotel room with her husband. White said that he told Peggy he did not have a weapon. She told him to meet her at the Logan Martin Dam.

A woman named Linda Vascocu testified that she was staying with Peggy on May 20, 1992, two days before the murder, when Betty and Peggy went to get ice cream and rent videos. White testified that was the night Peggy got out of Betty's black BMW and gave him Betty's .38-caliber gun at Logan Martin Dam. They left at 7:00 p.m. and picked up videos at 7:51 p.m., an employee testified. After the murder, the gun and the book, which had been checked out by Betty, were found at White's mobile home, a short distance from Peggy's church.

White then received a phone call early the next morning, on May 21, 1992. The caller, he said, was Betty Wilson, according to court records. That morning, White sat outside Dr. Wilson's office, waiting to kill him there, as he said Betty had instructed him to do. Although White said the sisters had given him a gun, he said he carried a rope he planned to use to kill the doctor. "A gun makes a lot of racket. Also, I'm kind of gun-shy from Vietnam," White later testified.

White soon decided that there were too many people at the office for him to kill Dr. Wilson there. He testified he found a payphone and called Peggy's house and spoke to Betty, who was staying there. White told her he needed money to stay the night in Huntsville to kill Dr. Wilson at home. Betty met White at the Chick-Fil-A restaurant at Parkway City Mall in Huntsville around noon and slipped him one hundred dollars in a bag, he later said. White said he then bought underwear and an overnight kit at a Kmart and checked into a Ramada Inn. After attempting to "jog" in blue jeans through Wilson's Boulder Circle neighborhood, White testified that Betty agreed to drive him there from the mall the day of the killing. So, they drove, with White crouched down in the floorboards, until they were safely parked in the garage.

Betty then allegedly left for her recovery meeting, while White waited for the doctor for two to three hours. "It seemed like a lifetime. I had been on drugs and drinking. The phone kept ringing, and I was real paranoid and scared. I almost left the crime undone," he testified. Dr. Wilson then surprised White as he walked out of a bedroom. White testified that he grabbed something—he didn't know what—and used it to bludgeon Dr. Wilson. "I hit him until he turned me loose. Then I left without knowing whether the doctor was dead." White didn't recall the stabbing. "Everything became foggy to me."

White testified that the next thing he remembered was being in the woods behind the Wilsons' home. He also testified that he was to pick up the other $2,500 from a bag in Peggy's garage on the Sunday after the murder. The money wasn't there, and when a neighbor of Peggy's saw White, he told them he had come by to pick up a ladder and some painting supplies that he had left in their garage.

"When do you tell the truth?" Cook asked, attacking White's credibility. "When I made peace with our God and decided to tell the truth," White replied. Cook tried to convince the jury that Betty was not a killer, even if jurors found her behavior distasteful. "This is not a case of maids, Mercedes, clothes and jewelry. She is not being tried for adultery. She is being tried for murder," Cook said in his closing remarks.

Betty Wilson (*center*) being escorted by Tuscaloosa County sheriff Ted Sexton (*left*) and an unidentified officer (*right*) from the courtroom after she was sentenced to life without parole. *Courtesy of the Alabama Department of Archives and History, donated by Alabama Media Group.*

Fry made his argument by banging a bat on a podium to show just what Dr. Wilson endured. "That would do it."

At the end of the six-day trial, it took the jury five hours to convict Betty of capital murder. "There was so much of it, time after time, we really couldn't come to any other verdict," said juror Mark Allison, according to AP. Betty's family sobbed as she was convicted. Cook said they'd appeal. "We'll win it." While being escorted out by deputies, Betty was asked if her story had been told during the trial. "No, it wasn't," she replied.

Though Dr. Wilson's family was pleased with the verdict, "it doesn't bring him back to his grandchildren," said his son Scott Wilson. "We miss our dad. He was a friend to a lot of people. He was a friend to us," said his son Stephen Wilson.

"They Just Knew the Truth When They Heard It"

While Betty's trial was held in Tuscaloosa to avoid publicity, Peggy's was held in Montgomery—the largest trial at the Montgomery courthouse since ex-governor Guy Hunt's ethics trial months earlier. "It's like I'm rushing to my destiny. It's in the hands of people who don't know me," Peggy told the *Huntsville Times* in an interview at a Montgomery motel. Vincent Elementary, she said, allowed her to work in the office, and she said that she was going to teach a third-grade class if acquitted. "I still have my birthday dinners with my girlfriends."

Assistant Alabama attorney general Don Valeska, however, said Peggy's role was a crucial one in the plot to murder Dr. Wilson. "If you take away this woman, you've got no killer. Jack Wilson's still alive," the *Montgomery Advertiser* quoted Valeska as saying.

Peggy's attorneys, however, told the jury that Betty wasn't convicted because of the strength of the evidence but because she had an affair with a Black man and battled alcoholism. "Some of the people thought Betty Wilson was less credible," said defense attorney Herman "Buck" Watson. Outside of court, three retired women who had met and become friends at Betty's trial compared notes at Peggy's trial, AP reported. Evelyn Creamer, Joann Burchfield and Mary Cooper smoked together during breaks and joked with attorneys. "We've seen this all before, and we know what they are going to say," Creamer said.

"He's on lithium, he's on Darvocet, he's smoking marijuana, he's drinking a case and a half of beer a day and a pint of whiskey. What can you believe?" Peggy's defense attorney, David Johnson, said of White. Peggy's husband, Wayne Lowe, testified they had tried to help White battle addiction. "We were trying to help him when we put him in touch with Betty." Peggy, unlike Betty, testified in her own defense, saying she had no indication that White had any infatuation with her.

A jury took two hours and ten minutes to acquit Peggy Lowe. "I asked the Lord to send me a good lawyer, and he did," Peggy said as she thanked Johnson. "I think they just knew the truth when they heard it." A juror who went unidentified by the *Montgomery Advertiser* later told the newspaper that Peggy "seemed sincere and very emotional." The juror felt the prosecutors focused too much on Betty. Valeska told me in an interview that Lowe's jury did not believe him because he was "outgodded" and because of the change of venue. "Tuscaloosa was a small community, and they understood what was going on.…Montgomery didn't. In their opinion, Betty Wilson did it, James White did it and Peggy Lowe was a religious woman."

To this day, Valeska says he believes Lowe manipulated White after a few minutes of sex, with a promise of more to follow if he did as she asked. Valeska said he believes Peggy manipulated Betty through some strange

Peggy Lowe talks to reporters after her acquittal. *Courtesy of the Alabama Department of Archives and History, donated by Alabama Media Group.*

family dynamic. "In a family, there may be one dominant sister and one subservient sister," Valeska theorized. "Why would Betty give up her great lifestyle? For her to give up her rich lifestyle, which she never had until she had her husband, only one person could have convinced her to do it.... That's the problem with the justice system; sometimes, the mastermind goes free. We thought no rational person could find this person not guilty."

"The Happiest Day of Her Life"

Betty's attorney Bobby Lee Cook, in 1993, said Peggy's acquittal would help with a retrial and still believed the verdict would be reversed. "Her affair with a Black man is what got her convicted," another of her defense attorneys, Jack Drake, argued to the Alabama Court of Criminal Appeals. Prosecutors noted that Betty frequently talked about her husband dying, even questioning, in 1986, a friend whose husband had taken his own life about whether the death was a murder and whether the friend could help Betty pull off the same thing with her own husband. Peggy attended the hearing.

It was around this time that White recanted his confession, which he later backed from. "I don't know what this means for her. In my heart, I've felt for two years we would one day see my mom home again," Betty's son Trey Taylor told the *Huntsville Times* in June 1994.

That July, Peggy started teaching again, AP reported. Some parents said they didn't want her teaching their kids, but many others supported Peggy, she said. "It was great to be back. The students have been by, some from the high school and middle school, that I taught."

In January 1995, Betty's conviction was upheld by the state supreme court, with the only call for a new trial coming from Justice Patterson.

In 1954, John Patterson was elected Alabama attorney general after his father was gunned down while battling corruption in Phenix City, then known as the "wickedest city in America." Elected governor four years later, Patterson presided over five executions in his single term in office. Forty years later, he was the only member of the state's highest court to challenge Wilson's conviction. Patterson wrote:

The following considerations strongly support the granting of a rehearing. The lack of corroboration of the testimony of the accomplice, James

White; the subsequent acquittal of the codefendant, who allegedly acted as a go-between in arranging the killing; the recantation of the testimony of the accomplice; and the question whether the trial court and the majority of this court gave proper weight to the recantation of White.

The case largely fell from the headlines until the tenth anniversary of the murder in 2002, which included coverage on *48 Hours* on CBS. Among those watching that night was Bill Campbell, an army contractor at Redstone Arsenal, the *Huntsville Times* reported. The Oklahoma native, a former Green Beret who served in Vietnam, became Betty's third husband in 2006. Betty and Bill were married at a ceremony at Tutwiler Prison. "The only stipulation is the cake has to be cut before it's brought into the prison," said Edward Blackwelder, a retired criminal justice professor at Wallace State-Hanceville, who served as the best man. "Somebody [once] brought in a cake and had a gun in it." The maid of honor was Peggy Peck, who was, by then, also married to her own third husband, a former University of Alabama professor.

"This is an injustice," Campbell said of Betty's conviction, which he also attributed to the interracial affair. Campbell visited Betty in prison twice a month before proposing. Brent Morrison, Betty's lawyer, was also there as the wedding party ate cake and drank Diet Mountain Dew and Diet Dr. Pepper. "I heard her say it was the happiest day of her life," Morrison said.

That same year, Peggy gave her first interview in fourteen years to WAFF TV's Georgi Bragg.

"Jack's Death Has Killed Life as We Know It"

"I met Mr. White at the elementary school where I was teaching. It was before school started in the spring or the summer. Mr. White had done some carpentry work for the teacher who occupied the classroom next door to mine," Peggy told Georgi. "So, when the next time he came up there, she introduced him to me. And I asked him if he would do the same thing in my room. And he agreed to do so."

Peggy said she hired White to do jobs at her own house and asked Betty to do the same, WAFF reported. "I asked Betty if she would help him, if she would let him do some of the work at her house, I remember very distinctly, she said, 'You know I will.'"

According to Peggy, White agreed to do some work in the Wilsons' kitchen but never showed up. "I was shocked that anybody was the murderer. I couldn't make it real. I couldn't connect Mr. White and Jack, and I couldn't understand if Mr. White had done this. Why Jack? Why would he kill Jack? I still can't make it real," Peggy told Bragg.

Nonetheless, Peggy pointed the finger at White—and the police. "I know that everything that Mr. White said is a lie. I know the police lied to us, manipulated us. I don't know why. I don't know why they would just take Mr. White's word for that. But I can tell you one thing, it could happen to you."

Peggy said Betty had no motive for killing her husband. "Betty had been divorced once. Jack had been divorced once. They didn't want out of their marriage. Betty and Jack were comfortable in the marriage," Peggy told WAFF. "I don't think they were unhappy. They laughed. Neither of them wanted out of it."

Bragg asked Peggy what the worst part of the whole ordeal was. "Jack's death has killed life as we know it, and we're all continually punished for something we didn't even know anything about because Mr. White was such a liar and such a contemptible soul that he was willing to risk Betty and me to save himself," Peggy replied.

When asked if White loved her, Peggy told Bragg, "I don't think that I am so stonewalled that I wouldn't have had some inkling that this man had some sort of affection for me. I think that's just something he made up, and that's just part of his story."

Betty Wilson in the state's most recently posted mugshot. *Courtesy of the Alabama Department of Corrections.*

Betty also gave WAFF a phone interview, saying she believed White "was given a deal he couldn't refuse. I can't blame him for trying to protect himself." But Betty maintained she was innocent. "Jack and I had an unusual marriage, to say the least. Even if I hadn't had an affair, it was still unusual. Jack insisted that I have affairs. I started drinking at that time. I stayed pretty much drunk for two years over that. I was unhappy; at one point, I told Jack if we didn't go to counseling together, if we didn't change our circumstances, I was going to divorce him," Betty told the station.

White told me prosecutors had no physical evidence against him and that, while he took Dr. Wilson's life, it was because he battled alcohol and drug addiction and because "a woman drove" him to it. In a letter that he wrote to me from prison, White used a story from the Bible to try to explain how Dr. Wilson ended up dead and he and Betty behind bars. "The rich, well-to-do, high-society folks carried a woman before Jesus and said this woman was caught in the very act of adultery. They said the law says we should stone her, but what do you say?" White wrote. "Well they all stood around for a little while then they ask Jesus again and Jesus's answer was, 'Who of you are without sin, let him cast the first stone.' Well, none of them could cast a stone, and they left one by one. But I can not [*sic*] change the way people think or feel, only God can do that. So, yes, I pray and ask God to touch Mr. Wilson's family and loved ones. I am truly sorry for what I did and pray that, someday, Mr. Wilson family will find compassion in their hearts to forgive."

11

LYNDA LYON BLOCK

Alabama's Antigovernment Cop Killer

For four tense hours on an October afternoon in 1993, Lynda Lyon Block and her common law husband, George Everette Sibley Jr., held police at bay in their red 1979 Ford Mustang, with her nine-year-old son in the backseat, near a Christmas tree farm in Notasulga. As dozens of officers, armed with rifles, surrounded the trio, Lynda yelled out that she would not be taken alive.

Lynda's son was quickly released from the car and taken by police as Lynda rattled off bizarre demands, asking for a TV set and an audience with the pope. Block said she was connected to David Koresh, the leader of the Branch Davidian religious sect who had died in a government raid in Waco, Texas, less than six months earlier. The deaths of eighty-two people in that Texas compound had perhaps cemented Lynda's beliefs that the federal government was out of control.

As the sun began to set on the rural, two-lane Wire Road, police prepared to use tear gas to force Lynda and George out of the car. Just then, the two surrendered to answer for gunning down Opelika police sergeant Roger Lamar Motley in a Walmart parking lot twelve miles away only hours earlier. "They weren't extremely rational," Auburn police chief Ed Downing told reporters after the arrests.

The October 4, 1993 murder of Sergeant Motley was one in a strange series of events that included the stabbing of Lynda's seventy-nine-year-old husband in Florida, a flood of angry faxes from antigovernment extremists and the final use to date of Alabama's electric chair—the Big Yellow Mama.

ASSOCIATED PRESS

Lynda Lyon Block and George Sibley Jr. surrender to police in Opelika on Monday.

Lynda Lyon Block and George Sibley surrender to police. *Courtesy of the Associated Press.*

"WE WILL NOT BE FORCED TO GO TO JAIL"

Lynda and Karl Block were self-employed publishers who married, even though Karl was twice Lynda's age. Flattery at the attention of a younger woman or grief over the death of his son in a 1974 car accident drove Karl to Lynda, according to the *Orlando Sentinel*. Lynda and the security broker, a military retiree, married and had a son together in 1984; she was in her mid-thirties at the time, and he was in his late sixties.

"His daughter, Marie, vividly remembers encountering her future stepmother in the early 1980s and recognizing her as a former high school classmate," the 2002 *Orlando Sentinel* report stated. "But the studious, brown-haired girl she had known at Edgewater High had been transformed into a boisterous woman, clattering with jewelry, long lacquered nails and hair dyed jet black. The only thing that went unchanged were her blue eyes,

141

so huge that she seemed to be transfixed in an expression of permanent surprise. Marie Block assumed Lynda Lyon was a gold digger and that the relationship would not last."

Born in Orlando on February 8, 1948, Lynda loved opera, sailing, motorcycles and poetry. She was active in Orlando community groups, including the local library, Cub Scouts and Humane Society. Her mother later told the *Orlando Sentinel* that Lynda spent her life trying to replace her father, Orlando businessman Frank Lyon, who died when she was a child. "She was always very idealistic. She was looking for Prince Charming." Lynda may have thought she met her "Prince Charming" when she was state vice-chair of the Libertarian Party of Florida and met George.

George Sibley was a mechanic who shared Lynda's views, including that the Constitution was being undermined by the United Nations and South Africa's diamond market. Born and raised in South Bend, Indiana, George moved to Orlando in 1976. Because of his slender face, Karl Block reportedly referred to George as "Ichabod Crane." Somewhere along the way, Lynda and George's shared hatred of the government blossomed into love for one another. Lynda called it "a true libertarian relationship of two highly intellectual, fiercely independent individualists who live passionately."

Lynda's relationship with Karl lasted until 1991, around the same time she began attending rallies by so-called patriot groups and publishing a magazine, *Liberatus*, where she wrote articles calling for people to renounce their driver's licenses and birth certificates. George Everette Sibley Jr. wrote a gun rights column for the magazine. "Only those who are armed with knowledge will know what to do. Everyone else will be at the mercy of the Feds when they come to confiscate everything they have, and their hearts will fail them," Block wrote in the final edition of *Liberatus* in August 1993.

In 1992, Karl petitioned a court to claim ownership of the Blocks' Orlando home. Lynda and George paid Karl a visit. They taped Karl's mouth shut and told him to drop the effort to get the house. "She held a knife real close to my chest and said, 'I mean business' and stabbed me," Karl said in an arrest report, according to the *Orlando Sentinel.*

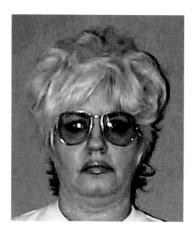

Lynda Lyon Block. *Courtesy of the Alabama Department of Corrections.*

"Our hell began, not with the agencies, but with Karl," she wrote. "Karl had sustained a cut from a small knife I had pulled out and held up as a warning, just as he had grabbed me. The cut was not large or deep, and when we offered to take him to a medical center, he refused, though he did allow us to bandage the cut." Lynda told George to close the one-inch knife wound to his chest with duct tape. A bloodied Karl walked to a drugstore to get himself a bandage when neighbors saw him and called for help. Lynda and George were charged with aggravated battery of someone over sixty-five; Karl Block died in 2000, at the age of eighty-seven.

While Karl declined to press charges, prosecutors pursued the case. Lynda and George agreed to plead guilty in exchange for six years of probation, rather than spend time in jail. Free on $7,500 bond each, their sentencing was set for September 7, 1993.

After agreeing to the plea, Lynda and George fired their court-appointed attorney and began filing court papers, arguing that the judge was an "illegal immigrant" because he occasionally used a "title of nobility"—the Honorable James Hauser. They also claimed Hauser had given secret hand signals to a court reporter to omit certain statements and was under government orders to jail them, despite the plea agreement. They attempted to withdraw their pleas, sending faxes to Hauser, the *Orlando Sentinel* and Orange County sheriff Kevin Beary, claiming they were coerced into pleading guilty. "Only very recently have I discovered that I do not have, nor have I ever had, a date of birth," Lynda wrote in one court filing. They did not show up for sentencing.

We "have now barricaded ourselves in our home here in Orlando, Florida, awaiting the inevitable attempt of the sheriff's deputies to surround us and take us by force," one fax read. "We will not live as slaves—but would rather die as free Americans," another stated. They faxed the *Orlando Sentinel*. "The police are here! God have mercy on us!" A deputy had knocked on the door at their home, but no one answered, and the authorities left because they did not have a search warrant. "They wanted a shootout at the OK Corral, but we didn't give it to them," an undercover Orange County sheriff's detective who worked on the case told the newspaper.

"We have every intention of standing and fighting this thing—in court. But we are both adamant in one thing: we will not be forced to go to jail for something we did not do," they wrote in a fax to Beary. In a September 18, 1993 fax from Newnan, Georgia, the couple said they had "run out of options" and were forced to run. Lynda claimed they fled Florida after she said a "friend in the sheriff's department" warned her police were "going to kill [her] and then say [she] shot at them first." The couple and their son stayed with friends in Georgia for weeks before deciding to hide out in Mobile and, along the way, get a motel room in Opelika.

Orlando bondsman Mike Parisciani and two bounty hunters had broken into and searched the couple's Florida home the day before the Newnan fax. "We found weapons, a couple thousand rounds of artillery and all kinds of stuff about white supremacist, Nazi and Klanlike groups," AP reported.

"Double Zero"

Two weeks later, Sergeant Motley made a routine stop at Walmart for supplies for the department. The thirty-eight-year-old had spent roughly half his life with the Opelika Police Department, working in dispatch, patrol, investigations and, by October 4, 1993, administration. Motley's work those days mostly involved making sure that the station and jail ran smoothly. The sergeant had recently given his bulletproof vest to a rookie officer because of a shortage in the department, and his car did not have a light rack.

Lynda and George stopped at a Big B Pharmacy at Opelika's Pepperell Corners Shopping Center so that Lynda could get a vitamin supplement and call a friend in Florida from a payphone. She ran out of change. After the couple drove away, Lynda remembered the friend had a tollfree 1-800 number, so they stopped at Walmart so she could use a payphone there.

Shortly after having lunch with his wife, Juanita, Motley was shopping for supplies for the jail when, around 1:15 p.m., a woman at Walmart told the officer about a little boy she heard call for help in a car in the parking lot; she was worried it was a family living in a car. Sergeant Motley circled the lot until he saw George Sibley with a child in a Mustang. George saw Sergeant Motley in his rearview mirror and got out of the car. "Motley asked Sibley for his driver's license. Sibley said he didn't need one. He was trying to explain why when Motley put his hand on his service revolver. Sibley reached into the car and pulled out a gun," the *Orlando Sentinel* reported. Motley took cover behind his cruiser as Sibley crouched by the bumper of the Mustang. Motley fired off three rounds, striking Sibley in the left arm.

People in the packed parking lot screamed, hid behind cars and made mad dashes to the store. "My first instinct was to protect my husband and son," Block later said. Lynda pulled a 9-mm Glock semiautomatic out of a holster behind her back, as Motley crouched beside his patrol car and began firing at the uniformed officer. "As I was shooting, something made him turn around and look at me with a look of total surprise." Lynda, later saying she did not think Motley had been shot, fired one or two more shots into his front and fired at him again as he tried to get into his car. Lynda said she fired those shots because she feared Motley was getting a shotgun. Lynda later wrote,

> *When I heard the popping noises, it took me a couple of seconds to realize it was gunfire. I cried, "Oh, God, no!" and dropping the phone, began running, ignoring the people scrambling for cover. I saw George standing between the rear of our car and the right side of the police car; he was holding his gun in his right hand, but his left arm was hanging strangely. Motley didn't see me approach, and just as I came to a stop, I pulled my own gun and shot several times. He turned to me in surprise, and as he did, one of my bullets struck him in the chest, and he fell backwards.*

Sergeant Motley was actually reaching into his car for his radio, and he managed to say, "double zero," the police code for officer in distress. He put the car in gear, and it coasted through the lot before hitting a parked car. Sergeant Motley died about an hour later at East Alabama Medical Center. He had been shot at least five times. A bulletproof vest wouldn't have saved his life, according to a statement made by Opelika police chief Tommy Mangham to reporters. "The weapons used were so powerful it wouldn't have made any difference."

As the shooting ended, Lynda ran to the Mustang. George told her he was going to give the officer the car's paperwork and was afraid Motley was about to kill him. "I couldn't just stand there and let him shoot me," Lynda wrote George told her. "George is the most honest person I know. He would not have placed himself or us in danger. He took the law seriously. He was never the showoff gunslinger type and would walk away before being drawn into a fight." Lynda wrote that she told George she believed him but that they had to get away.

The Mustang, which bore a bumper sticker that said, "A woman raped is a woman without a gun," was spotted several minutes after the shooting, just south of Auburn. As the bleeding man fled police at speeds of more than one hundred miles per hour, Lynda tried to calm her son.

As they saw twenty police cars on a country roadblock, Lynda said she told George, "I guess this is it, isn't it?" George merely nodded. Lynda said she told her son to be a good boy and that the police would take care of him.

She said she gave her son a last kiss and studied the features of a face she might never see again. Lynda made sure police could see her gun, so they knew they were in for a gunfight or double suicide if they swarmed the car.

"Let's not have another Waco happen here," Lynda told a police negotiator. The officer asked, "What's Waco?" Lynda and George, losing blood, weighed their options for four hours. "My religious belief is that suicide is wrong, but now, I was faced with the total hopelessness of our situation," she wrote. She said George suggested she surrender while he put a bullet in his head. Lynda told George that they would either die there together or surrender together. They clasped their blood-soaked hands, shared a final kiss and dropped their guns. The car contained more than one thousand rounds of ammo, a camouflage M-14 rifle with scope, an SKS Chinese assault rifle and multiple handguns and knives.

"I didn't intend to kill the officer. I didn't want that," Lynda said after her arrest. It was not clear if Lynda's gun or Sibley's Russian-made Norinco semiautomatic pistol killed Motley. Lynda most likely fired the fatal shot, according to court records.

His encounter with Lynda and George was the first time Sergeant Motley had ever fired his service revolver in the line of duty.

"You Have Changed Me Forever"

Because of a fear that Lynda and George were connected to other violent extremists, Opelika officers, after the shooting, patrolled in unmarked cars. Some members of the antigovernment network that George and Lynda were plugged into via fax machine were quick to denounce the shooting.

"I'm shocked," Pat Sutton, a retired deputy sheriff who lived outside of Jacksonville, Florida, told the *Montgomery Advertiser*. "An aggravated battery charge resulting from a divorce is not that unusual. It's not something you'd shoot a police officer over. It just doesn't fit." Sutton had tried to convince Lynda not to leave Orlando, to work the system and send her faxes. "What they did was unacceptable….There has to be a line you cannot cross."

"Any violence of any kind is stupid. What they were talking about was totally irrational," Ken Vardon, a founder of American Patriot Fax Network, told the newspaper. "She believed the state didn't have the authority to intervene in a God-given right," said Gerry Hughes, a Lakeland, Florida radio host who had interviewed Lynda.

"They were decent, thoughtful, caring people. What changed? I don't know," said Gary Hunt, an activist who drove a minivan to Opelika from Waco to support the couple. After all, they had come to his defense. In Waco, Hunt had offered to have power of attorney for Koresh, which NPR reported Koresh signaled he agreed to by waving a satellite dish from the compound. Hunt, a former land surveyor who worked with the Phoenix-based group Outpost of Freedom, often warned of a coming war with the government. Hunt feared he had been spied on in Waco and asked armed supporters to meet him when he arrived at the Orlando airport in case the government tried to kill him. "After Waco, what was just a theory became a reality," Hunt later told the *Orlando Sentinel*.

Lynda and George were among those who were waiting to greet Hunt in Florida. He returned the favor after Motley's murder, sending faxes in support of the couple, saying they were defending themselves from an illegal arrest. "The concept of liberty was very important to the founding fathers, and the concept cannot be taken away just because someone works for the government," Hunt wrote. In 2017, a federal judge held Hunt in contempt for a blog post that divulged the names of FBI informants linked to an investigation of the armed takeover of the Malheur National Wildlife Refuge in Oregon.

While awaiting trial, George and Lynda supposedly swapped love letters. "You have changed me forever, Lynda, and for the better. I am a whole and complete man with you, and I know that even if we can't communicate for a while that you will never forsake me and will always love me," George wrote. "I tried to picture you in my mind, and the picture of you I love best is how you look in jeans, your snug-fitting shirt, and your leather jacket. With your tall, slim stature and your wavy hair, you looked so incredibly elegant and handsome. I love your boyish smile and your direct, intense gaze," Lynda wrote to him.

"Putting Her Own Head in a Noose"

With his police hat and an Atlanta Braves cap resting on his casket, Sergeant Motley was given a hero's sendoff before he was buried in Wing, a small town near Andalusia. He was remembered as a man who sent his wife flowers "just because." His widow received a note from a man who had been a prisoner in the Opelika jail that said Motley always treated him with kindness.

Police officers grieve

Associated Press

Opelika police officers Keith Grohke, right, and Brian McDonough wipe their tears as they leave the funeral for fellow officer Sgt. Roger L. Motley Thursday in Wing, Ala. Motley was gunned down in an area parking lot Monday morning and died later from his wounds at a hospital.

Opelika police officers cry at the funeral of Sergeant Roger Motley. *Courtesy of the Associated Press.*

Prosecutors, meanwhile, were preparing to do their damnedest to put Lynda and George on Alabama's death row. George was the first to be tried for capital murder in Motley's death. When Lynda testified at his trial, she practically convicted herself. "I don't think there's ever been a criminal case this big in the history of the county," said George's attorney, Dan McKeever, who helped prosecute Ted Bundy in Florida. "Everyone needs to understand how careful we need to be that it not become a circus."

It became a circus.

George sent a confession from jail to his supporters, arguing that the shooting was justified. They shared it with a newspaper. The judge refused

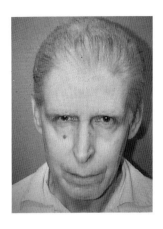

George Sibley. *Courtesy of the Alabama Department of Corrections.*

to let McKeever step down from the case when he complained that Sibley inundated him with court cases from the 1800s he said supported his defense. "It's as if they are literally patriots who are trying to start a new world government," McKeever said at the time. "He is a tremendously intelligent person, but what is in front of him is a death penalty case."

As Lee County district attorney Ron Myers made his closing argument, George said he wanted Lynda to testify, despite objections from Myers and Lynda's court-appointed lawyer, Roger Pierce. Judge Robert Harper discussed it with the jury outside of the courtroom and then brought Lynda in from a jail cell downstairs.

Harper warned Lynda's lawyer that she "may well be putting her own head in a noose," since the testimony could be used in her trial. She said they fired in self-defense and that she had been taught by a former Green Beret in 1992 to only "shoot to kill."

The jury took less than an hour to convict Sibley and ninety minutes to recommend execution. Instead of pleading for lenience, George said he was defending himself and was within his rights. However, he said he did not want to be executed. "At least, if I'm still alive, I would have a chance at legal recourse. If I'm dead, I don't."

When the judge accepted the jury's death sentence recommendation, Sibley again protested that he was innocent and said McKeever gave him incompetent representation. "The reality of our situation only hit me then, when they took George away to Death Row," Lynda wrote. "You carried yourself proudly in the courtroom, and this is what the jury hated. They wanted submissive, emotional groveling. They wanted pained expressions of remorse. You are truly a brave man, Sweetheart, and I am honored to be your wife," she wrote to George from jail. She also wrote that death would be better than life behind bars.

Life in prison is not "life." It is living hell for someone like you or me. Living in a caged existence where you are told what to eat, what to wear, where to sleep, when to sit or stand; where your meager belongings are regularly searched, where even your body is inspected, where the only intellectual stimulation you receive is what they allow—what kind of life is that?

"I PRAYED THAT THEY WOULD GIVE ME DEATH"

Lynda declared that she wished to represent herself as she went on trial in 1994. She argued that Alabama had no right to try her because the state had not officially rejoined the Union after the Civil War. She also argued self-defense and cited an unratified 1811 Constitutional amendment limiting the power of public employees. "My lawyers and I argued at every meeting because they refused to even consider the Constitutional issues," she wrote. "I had no choice but to fire these useless attorneys and conduct my own trial." Lynda said she wasn't interested in saving her life—she wanted acquittal or death.

Lynda later said she was prohibited from bringing up records that she said described Motley as a "bad cop" and a wife beater. His wife has said the sergeant was kind and patient. A news report said that Motley's most serious trouble on the job was a fender-bender in his police car.

The jury took two hours to convict Lynda and, by a 10–2 vote, recommend the death penalty, which the judge accepted. "The trial was a play, scripted by the judge, the prosecutor," Lynda wrote. "I had little chance, and I knew it."

Lynda said she remained stoic as the verdict was read. She wrote,

> I forced myself to sit perfectly still, emotionless, while realizing that the people of Alabama wanted to kill me for choosing to defend my husband's life....No one can possibly imagine being alone in a courtroom, feeling the eyes of everyone else upon you waiting for your reaction to the news that they were going to put you to death in a most horrible manner....I prayed that they would give me death. If George and I were both on death row, we could join our appeal and fight together.

Lynda arrived at Tutwiler Prison on December 21, 1994, where she remained for nearly seven and a half years. Lynda kept her hair dyed blond and decorated her cell with pictures of Abraham Lincoln. Lynda also researched what happened to people in the electric chair, the *Orlando Sentinel* reported. "Your eyeballs explode," she wrote. "They put a hood over your face because the jolt of 20,000 volts causes your face to contort and your eyeballs to explode."

She was scheduled to die on April 19, 2002, the anniversary of the Waco raid and the 1995 Oklahoma City bombing. The Alabama Supreme Court delayed the execution, although no one had requested the change, and the court offered no reason for the delay. Juanita Motley told journalists that she had her suspicions behind the delay. "I don't want to make a martyr out of her. If that's the reason, I prefer it to be May 10."

Lynda, meanwhile, refused lawyers or appeal efforts, according to a two-paragraph note released by supporters to the AP. "I refuse ANY actions by attorneys or groups of attorneys, either hired by others or on their own initiative, to file documents on my behalf as a 'last ditch' effort to stay execution."

"I tried my best to save her life," her appeals attorney, W. David Nichols, told the *Orlando Sentinel*. "The warden took me down to her cell and said, 'Lynda, they're trying to fry you. You ought to talk to this boy. He wants to help.' But she wasn't interested."

Governor Don Siegelman rejected Lynda's plea for clemency. "The evidence during the trial was overwhelming. There are no mitigating circumstances whatsoever." Siegelman, who held four of the state's highest elected offices, in 2012, was sent to federal prison after a bribery case that he argues was driven by politics. He was released in 2017. Eight Alabama inmates were executed in the three years that Siegelman was governor.

As her execution neared, in a two-page handwritten note, Lynda said she was denied records that proved Motley's "known adversarial character"; she also said that she was denied access to a law library and that the prosecutor directed witnesses with head shakes and hand motions. She also claimed that the judge and prosecutor made witnesses and evidence "disappear." Sergeant Motley's widow called the claims ridiculous.

Lynda was denied an interview with WSFA-TV. The Alabama Department of Corrections cited security reasons for this denial. Prison commissioner Mike Haley said he did not want to bring "any recognition to Ms. Block or dishonor Sgt. Motley or his badge." Juanita disagreed with his decision at first, saying supporters would call the denial of an interview another government conspiracy. "They are playing into her hands." She later changed her mind, saying, "The TV interview would be her trying to promote her political beliefs and defame my husband."

Juanita struggled with whether or not to witness the execution. "I'm not sure I want to have that image with me the rest of my life," she told the *Montgomery Advertiser*. "Hatred and bitterness were poisoning my life. I had to learn to put that down," she said of the first few years after the murder. She said she preferred, instead, to teach her grandkids about the Papa Roger they would never meet. Juanita, however, told the newspaper she might watch the execution because Lynda talked about Roger being

People gather outside the governor's mansion in Montgomery shortly before midnight Thursday to hold a vigil for Lynda Lyon Block, who was soon to be executed in Atmore.

sentiments run strong and she is   she was concerned about her ev-   has to work out her peace with

Protesters gather outside of the governor's mansion before the execution of Lynda Lyon Block. *Courtesy of the* Montgomery Advertiser.

"aggressive." "I don't think she has an ounce of humanity in her. I am a compassionate person. If I had seen some sympathy for the victim in all of this, I wouldn't feel the need to see this finished," Juanita said at the time.

Still, her heart went out to Lynda's mother, who had written Juanita a card after the murder, saying her daughter wasn't raised that way. She said she was raised in a Christian home and that she was sorry for what Sergeant Motley's family was going through. She signed it "Lynda's Mom." "I just can't get her off my mind," Juanita told the newspaper. "To know the exact moment your daughter is going to die must be unbearable."

Roger's mother, Anne Motley, didn't seem to share Juanita's reluctance to watch the execution, telling reporters, "The Bible says when a murder happens and a person has no sorrow, they are to be immediately executed."

When Lynda was taken from Tutwiler to Atmore's Holman Prison, where the death chamber is located, George Sibley was temporarily taken from

Holman to Bessemer's Donaldson Prison, apparently to keep them from being in the same prison at the same time.

Even Alabama's staunchest death penalty opponents seemed reluctant to help Lynda. "Normally, I could tell you if we have something going on and what we believe will happen, but this is a very complicated situation," Bryan Stevenson of the Equal Justice Initiative (EJI) told a newspaper when asked if the EJI would intervene. Stevenson has helped exonerate multiple death row inmates, and his memoir was made into the 2019 film *Just Mercy*. In Europe, Lynda was seen as a "political prisoner," according to prison commissioner Haley.

"ROGER'S GRANDCHILDREN ARE GROWING UP WITHOUT HIM"

The fifty-four-year-old Lynda was scheduled to be executed at 12:01 a.m. on Friday, May 10, 2002. Siegelman had recently signed into law a bill that allowed inmates to choose lethal injection over the electric chair. That law did not take effect until July 1, 2002, so Lynda was bound for Big Yellow Mama.

She started fasting on milk and water on Tuesday for religious reasons, met with a former chaplain and friends from Orlando and took no final meal. She entered the death chamber with her head shaved, wearing mascara and pink lipstick. Juanita Motley was there in the witness chamber. "I went as far as I could with this. I saw Lynda," she later told the *Montgomery Advertiser*. "I asked an officer to take me out." Still, she said she was sad that none of Lynda's family members were there for her final moments. "It seems to me that no one cared. I feel very sorry for her. It must have been a very lonely time that she spent in prison....I feel that the family members of Lynda are also victims. Grief and loss know no bounds." It was reported Lynda had asked her family to not witness the execution.

In handwritten instructions, Lynda left her TV, microwave, fan, lamp and typewriter to Tutwiler "for inmates' use as the authorities see fit." She wrote that she wanted no autopsy because it "is against my religious beliefs to desecrate a body."

Lynda seemed to mouth a silent prayer before the hood went on, and she kept her eyes open. "She closed them a couple of times and took long, deep breaths, like she was trying to calm herself," said Dave Bryan of the AP. "She was just wide-eyed, looking straight ahead. It was unsettling," said Jason

State executes Block
First woman to die in chair since 1957

By Todd Kleffman
Montgomery Advertiser

Alabama executed Lynda Lyon Block at 12:01 a.m. Friday for her role in killing Opelika Police Sgt. Roger Motley in 1993.

Block died at 12:10 a.m. Friday, said John Hamm, Department of Corrections spokesman.

She is the first woman executed in the state since 1957.

Department of Corrections Commissioner Michael Haley said Block walked willingly to the execution chamber and displayed no emotion to the very end.

"She had a very blank, emotionless stare," Haley said. "The execution was routine. There was never any unexpected incidents."

Block declined the offer to make a final statement.

An emotional Juanita Motley entered the witness room but asked to be removed shortly before Block was executed.

"I went as far as I could with this," the police officer's widow said. "I saw Lynda, but when they pulled back the blind to put the hood over her face, I asked an officer to take me out.

Motley said she felt no closure from Block's death and expressed compassion for her family and friends.

"My heart goes out to them," she said. "May God grant them the peace of mind and stamina needed in the days ahead."

Block wore a prison outfit, with her shaved head covered by a black hood. She wore light makeup, with mascara and a pale shade of pink lipstick.

There were no last-minute appeals from Block. There also were limited protests Thursday night leading up to the execution. About nine people kept silent vigil at the Alabama governor's mansion on South Perry Street in Montgomery just before midnight. It was not confirmed whether Gov. Don Siegelman was in residence.

Block and her common-law husband, George Sibley, were both convicted for killing Motley during a gun battle in a Wal-Mart parking lot. She was convicted of capital murder in 1994 along with Sibley, who remains on death row.

Block may be the last per-

Todd Van Emst Advertiser

From left, Jason Perkins, his mother, Juanita Motley, and her daughter, Delisa Perkins, speak before the execution of Lynda Lyon Block, who was convicted of killing Juanita Motley's husband.

Victim's relatives greet solemn sunset

By Todd Kleffman
Montgomery Advertiser

The sun went down Thursday evening on the life of Lynda Lyon Block, leaving a lightly painted pink sky over Holman Prison before fading to black.

And silence.

From a distance cows could be heard lowing in the fields in front of the prison where Block would be executed just after the stroke of midnight.

It wasn't known if Block took in that last sunset. She could have, if she had wanted. Prison officials try to be as accommodating as they can during those last hours, said John Hamm, associated commissioner of the state Department of Corrections.

Three miles away at the Best Western in Atmore, family, friends and fellow officers of slain Opelika Police Sgt. Roger Motley gath-

George Sibley — anti-government zealots on the run from Florida authorities — in the parking lot of the Opelika Wal-Mart. For that crime, Block would become the first woman put to death in Alabama since 1957.

Sibley remains on death row awaiting an execution date.

"It's been a long eight-and-a-half years," said Anne Motley, who was wearing the Medal of Honor her son received from the Fraternal Order of Police.

"My son hasn't been able to breathe and see the sunshine. She has. I think now is the time to take all that away from her and have her pay for her sins."

Block, 54, refused to indulge in the traditional last meal afforded those about to die. For spiritual reasons, Block began a fast on Tuesday and only consumed milk and water, Hamm said.

Todd Van Emst Advertiser

Alabama Department of Corrections Commissioner Mike Haley talks at a news conference early Friday after the execution of Lynda Lyon Block, the first woman to die in Alabama's electric chair since 1957.

The family of Sergeant Roger Motley talks to reporters before the execution of Lynda Lyon Block. *Courtesy of the* Montgomery Advertiser.

Wheeler of **WKRG-TV** in Mobile. "About 12:01, there was a jolt. Her body tensed up. Steam rose up from the top of her head," Wheeler said. The final surge lasted two minutes, and she was pronounced dead at 12:10 a.m. As of this writing, Lynda was the last person to die in Alabama's electric chair. She was the 177th person to die there since the state switched from hanging to electrocution in 1927.

Three years and eight lethal injections later, George, on August 4, 2005, faced his own execution and joined Lynda in death. The sixty-two-year-old was pronounced dead at 6:26 p.m., after becoming the ninth person in Alabama to be executed with poison. "Everyone who is doing this to me is guilty of a murder," he said before his execution.

In the decades since Sergeant Motley's death, Juanita has been left with the void that was created by his murder. "Mine and Roger's grandchildren are growing up without him. We now have great-grandchildren who will never meet him," she told me. Juanita Motley calls the death penalty a "necessary evil" in today's world and still cannot fathom the bizarre ideology embraced by the couple who killed her husband. "It's just unbelievable that someone in this day and time would have those beliefs."

Visit us at
www.historypress.com